UNDERSTANDING SOMALIA:

GUIDE TO CULTURE, HISTORY AND SOCIAL INSTITUTIONS

D0912548

I.M. Lewis

HAAN Associates, London

First Edition published by L.S.E., London, 1981

Second Edition 1993
Reprinted 1995
ISBN 1 874209 41 3
Published by HAAN Associates, P.O. Box 607,
London SW16 1EB.

Printed in Great Britain by
Hobbs the Printers Ltd, Totton, Hampshire SO40 3YS

Cover design by HAAN Graphics; line drawing
from an early 1900s photograph of Seyyid
Mohamed Abdille Hassan's fort at Taleh.

PREFACE

This social anthropological overview of the Somali people, based on research since the 1950s, is intended to provide a brief introduction to key features of Somali culture and institutions. It was originally written for USAID in 1978 and the text has now been revised and up-dated for wider circulation. The book is divided into sections with self-explanatory headings. The summary of post-independence history is designed to give the reader some familiarity and insight into the recent political past which is very relevant to the present. I have tried also to emphasise the pervasive influence in the contemporary structure of Somalia of the traditional nomadic background. This brief introduction to a very complex people and their country is, of course, no substitute for firsthand experience. I hope, however, that it may help to make such experience informed and fruitful.

I. M. Lewis
London School of Economics and Political Science
June 1993

Books by the same Author

Peoples of the Horn of Africa (1955, 1969)

A Pastoral Democracy (1962, 1982; Italian edition 1984)

Marriage and the Family in Northern Somaliland (1962)

Somali Poetry (with B.W. Andrzejewski, 1964)

A Modern History of Somalia: from Nation to State (1965,1982,1988)

Islam in Tropical Africa (ed. 1966,1982)

History and Social Anthropology (ed. 1968, 1972)

Ecstatic Religion (1971, 1978; Dutch edition 1972;

Portuguese edition 1974; Italian edition 1987; Chinese edition 1987)

Social Anthropology in Perspective (1976, 1986)

Symbols and Sentiments (1977)

Somali Culture, History and Social Institutions (1981)

Atlas of Mankind (ed. with others, 1982)

Nationalism and Self-Determination in the Horn of Africa (ed. 1983)

Religion in Context: Cults and Charisma (1986, German edition 1989)

O Islamismo ao sul do Saara (Lisbon 1986)

Blueprint for a Socio-Demographic Survey and re-Enumeration of the
Refugee Camp Population in the Somali Democratic Republic (ed. 1986)

Acquiring Culture: Cross-Cultural Studies in Child Development
(ed. with other, 1988)

Women's Medicine: the Zar/Bori Cult in Africa and Beyond (ed. 1991)

Blood and Bone: the Call of Kinship in Somali Culture (1993)

CONTENTS

Part One: The Social Setting

Part Two: Pre- and Post-Colonial History

Part Three: Society and Economy

Part Four: War and Famine

Diagrams, Tables and Maps

Part One: The Social Setting

UNDERSTANDING SOMALIA:

GUIDE TO CULTURE, HISTORY AND SOCIAL INSTITUTIONS

1. The Somali Ethnic Region

With a total population of some 5 million, the Somali form a single ethnic unit in the Horn of Africa stretching from the Awash valley in the north to beyond the Tana River in Northern Kenya in the south. Ethnically, in terms of linguistic and cultural affiliation, they belong to the Cushitic-speaking family. This includes the neighbouring Afar (or Danakil—or Oodali—as the Somalis call them) of Djibouti, Eritrea and the Awash Valley, and the Oromo and Borana Galla* of Ethiopia and Northern Kenya.

2. Migration and the Islamic Tradition

With a long tradition of trading connexions with the Arabian Peninsula, the Somalis were early converted to Islam and remain staunch Muslims (Sunnis, of the Sha'afi-ite). This is reflected in the traditional practice of tracing descent from illustrious Arab ancestors connected with the family of the Prophet Mohamed. Its modern expression can be seen in Somalia's membership, since 1974, of the Arab League.

Over the centuries there has been a general drift of population from north to south. One of the major routes has been from the north-east coast of Sanag Region—where some of the

* This cultural connection is particularly strong in the case of the Muslim Oromo, e.g., the Arussi of Bali province of Ethiopia whose anti-Ethiopian liberation movement was associated with the Western Somali Liberation Front. This is reflected in the name 'Somali Abo' applied by Somalis to these Muslim Arussi. The term 'Galla' applied to the Oromo (and Borana) peoples by the Amharas has derogatory connotations and is strongly repudiated today.

founders of the major clan groupings are buried. Another major route that recurs frequently in the oral tradition is by way of the ancient Islamic citadel of Harar where the ancestors of other Somali groups are buried.

The establishment about one thousand years ago of Arab and Persian trading settlements at such coastal centres as Zeila in the north, on the trade route to Harar, and Mogadishu, Brava and Merca in the south, gave an additional impetus to these population movements, reinforcing the Islamic identity of the Somali people.

As Muslims, the Somalis played an important role in the protracted 'holy wars' *(Jihads)* which raged in the late Middle Ages between Christian Ethiopia and the surrounding Islamic sultanates. At their peak in the 16th century, from his base in Harar, the great Islamic leader Ahmad Gurey ('Ahmad the left-handed') briefly conquered much of the central Abyssinian highlands. Somali participation in these wars remains a vivid part of folk consciousness in the region, particularly since the Islamic hero's lieutenant was a Somali of the same name. These two figures are often confused in the oral tradition.

The traditional centres of Islam, partly connected with Arab immigration and settlement, are the towns of Harar in the north-west highlands, its ancient port Zeila, and in the south, Mogadishu (known to Somalis as 'Hamar' after one of the two early divisions of the city), Merca, and Brava—whose ancient city population speak a Swahili-related dialect called 'Chimbalazi'. The inhabitants of Brava are noted for their skills in learning foreign languages. A significant number of Protocol officials in Somali governments since independence have been drawn from this town.

3. The Somali Nation and its Traditional Divisions

The Somali are essentially a pastoral nomadic people, herding camels (the traditional prestige wealth), sheep and goats and in favourable regions, cattle. Between 60% and 70% of the population are nomadic or have nomadic affiliation, while many of the remainder who cultivate also keep livestock.

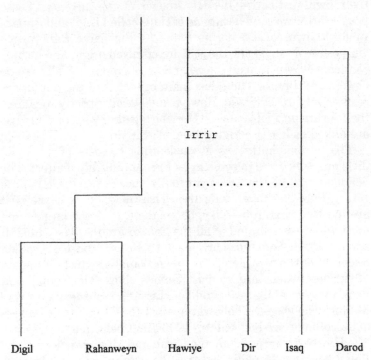

Legendary Arabian Ancestry

Irrir

Digil   Rahanweyn   Hawiye   Dir   Isaq   Darod

The distinction between nomad and cultivator coincides roughly with the most marked internal division in the Somali nation. The fertile area between the Shebelle and Juba Rivers is occupied mainly by cultivators who, while they generally understand the standard spoken Somali current elsewhere, speak their own distinctive dialect, known as *Af-maymay*. These people form two confederations of clans called Digil and Rahanweyn, known collectively as Sab.* As the name Rahanweyn ('large crowd') suggests, the Sab are of mixed origin and include elements drawn from all the other Somali groups as well as some Oromo and Bantu. The other main branches of the nation are respectively the Dir, Isaq, Hawiye and Darod. Strictly speaking, the Isaq are an offshoot of the Dir who together with the Hawiye, are linked as Irir at a higher level of grouping.

The Somali nation as a whole thus consists of six main divisions which are to some extent geographically distinct. The headquarters of the Dir, principally the Esa and Gadabursi clans, are in the Harar-Zeila area. Their neighbours in the west are the Isaq who in turn neighbour the Darod, the largest and most widely distributed of all the Somali groups. They inhabit north-eastern Somalia, north-eastern Kenya and the Ogaden region of eastern Ethiopia (Western Somalia) which is named after one of their largest most famous clans. The Somali folk hero, Seyyid Mohamed Abdille Hassan, the so-called 'Mad Mullah' who waged a holy war against the Christian colonisers of his country (see below) from 1900-1920, belonged to this clan. The Hawiye in turn occupy the Hiran and Mudug regions of the Republic, and Benadir, where the capital city is located. Mogadishu or Hamar, however, as an ancient trading port and later the country's capital was always cosmopolitan in composition, containing representatives of all Somali groups in addition to its own distinctive Arabized city populations known as *Reer*** Hamar, and also Asharaf. Hawiye clans stretch across the

---

* The term 'Sab' is traditionally used in northern Somalia to refer to disadvantaged minority specialist groups such as the Midgans (hunters and leather-workers) Tumals (blacksmiths) and Yibirs (itinerant hunters and pedlars)

** The term *Reer* means group or people.

Shebelle River into the region occupied by the Digil and Rahanweyn, where some of them have become cultivators. They occur again, along with various Darod nomadic clans, in the the trans-Juba region and north-eastern Kenya.

4. Family organisation

The Somalis are traditionally polygynous, marrying, according to the Islamic code, a maximum of four wives at any one time. The number of wives a man has varies generally with age: seniority being associated with more wives. The actual incidence of polygyny varies widely: both amongst the pastoral nomads and the southern Digil and Rahanweyn the majority of men will probably have had at least two wives at some point in their lives. The rich and successful will usually have four. Since marriage is extremely unstable, with a high frequency of divorce, the number of marriages contracted in the course of the average man's life is actually often far higher than these statements would indicate. A significantly high proportion of the male population will have contracted half a dozen marriages or more before they die: others will have contracted many more than this. The primary aim of marriage is to produce children, especially male heirs who will add strength and honour to their father's lineage and enhance his reputation and status. There are elders with 100 or more living descendants. In a harsh environment with a high infant mortality rate and climatic uncertainties, the Somalis recognise that, as with their livestock husbandry, they overproduce their human population to allow for the effects of natural hazards. Since at all levels in the population, fighting strength and political muscle are a matter of force of numbers, optimum size is the constant goal. These attitudes, widely prevalent in the population, are not conducive to birth control schemes.

In the polygynous family, each wife and her children form a separate unit with their own dwelling and small stock (sheep and goats). In the case of cultivators, if a man has ample land, it is divided into separate plots: if land is scarce the wives work in the same plot, but the harvest is divided between them. Each uterine family *(haas* or *raas)* within the polygynous family *(haasas* or *raasas)* is called *bah*, its children being full siblings but only paternal half-siblings to the children of other families. The first wife is the senior *(bahweyn* or *minweyn)*, her children being the firstborn *('urad)*; she heads the family of wives and, traditionally, keeps the keys of the family moneybox. Since, although Islam enjoins them to treat their wives equally, men tend to favour the youngest most physically attractive marriage partner, there is much jealousy and friction between co-wives and their children. Indeed the word co-wife *(dangalo)* also means jealousy.

The relative seniority of wives and their children is reflected in the precedence of the first wife's family in the distribution of the joint family income and in inheritance rights. In the traditional Islamic inheritance rules, female heirs have reduced rights to male heirs. In practice amongst the Somali, although women might inherit housing, land and small stock, they rarely acquired possession of camels which are treated as a male preserve. A new family law *(heerka qoyska)* introduced by the Siyad regime in 1975 gave female heirs the same rights as male heirs, though the extent to which this new dispensation was practised among pastoral nomads was hard to gauge. Certainly male superiority is still taken for granted, men regularly walking before their wives who walk at a respectful distance behind.

The sexual division of labour, with women assigned the husbandry of sheep and goats while men deal with grazing camels, emphasises these chauvinist attitudes which are further reinforced in the machismo honour code, stressing vulnerability and chastity of women. However, particularly amongst the nomads, women are not veiled (as some used to be in towns) and enjoy considerable freedom of movement and independence in the management of sheep and goats. Somali women are often forceful characters who perhaps exercise more influence than appears on the surface.

5. Marriage arrangements

Although, traditionally, marriages were ideally arranged by the elder kinsmen of the spouses, elopement seems to have been a common way of avoiding such arranged matches. The urban trend towards allowing individuals to choose their own partners, encouraged by the 'revolutionary-period' government of the seventies and eighties, seemed also to affect marriage patterns in the interior.

Historically, marriage amongst the nomads (with some exception in the case of the Mijerteyn clansmen) was usually outside the *diya*-paying group, the basic political unit. This reflected the political significance of marriage as an alliance between potentially hostile groups and sometimes included in peace terms. This political aspect inspired the main marriage payments from the groom's group to the wife's *(yarad)* and the return gift *(dibaad)* made at or after the actual wedding. These transactions involve traditionally large numbers of livestock, especially camels, and other items of prestige wealth, including money. The return presents brought by the bride from her kin include the marriage house *(aros*)* and, typically, a flock of sheep and goats to supply milk to the children of the union and burden camels to transport the family from place to place. The crucial Islamic element uniting the couple as man and wife is the *mahar,* a witnessed contract, according to which the groom undertakes to pay his wife a present of an agreed value in cash or kind. Despite its religious significance, this is often only actually paid on divorce, and so acts as a divorce surety for the wife—although its material value may be slight.

Amongst the southern cultivating Somali (Digil and Rahanweyn) marriage is a less costly undertaking. Here the main transaction is the *mahar,* and it is usually the groom's rather than bride's family who supply the matrimonial house. Marriage partners are at the same time not chosen from remote groups. Indeed there is a strong preference for marriage with a paternal or maternal cousin. This may help to integrate the heterogeneous Digil and Rahanweyn clans which consist of so many different elements. Amongst pastoralists and cultivators, though more in the case of the former, if a husband dies his widow may be inherited by the deceased husband's brother or

---

* This word is also used to denote the marriage ceremony

other close relative. This widow inheritance is called *dumaal.* Similarly, a widower has some entitlement to a replacement bride *(higsiisan).* These practices underline the corporate rather than purely personal nature of marriage as an alliance, especially among the pastoral nomads.

6. Religion and General Cultural Characteristics

The Somalis are firmly attached to Islam and divided into three main denominations: the Qadiriya, the Ahmadiya, and its derivative the Salihiya. These are Sufi or mystical brotherhoods found throughout the Muslim world, the Qadiriya being the oldest and least puritanical. The Salihiya is a nineteenth century reformist movement, owing its importance in Somalia to the fact that the national hero, Seyyid Mohamed Abdille Hassan waged his crusade against the Christian colonisers under its banner. The Qadiriya has, however, a larger number of followers. Few Somalis are formal initiates of these religious movements. Their founders have, however, been assimilated into the Somali calendar of saints (including local clan founders like Sheikhs Darod and Isaq) and their sheikhs act as local religious leaders and teachers. In the late 1980s and early 1990s, missionaries with Saudi, Sudanese or Iranian connections and resources (including arms in some cases) began to compete for followers amongst those who felt alienated by the terrible scourges their country had endured.

Here we encounter the complementary relationship which Somalis see between the laiety and men of God. This is expressed traditionally in the phrase 'man of God (i.e. priest/sheikh) and warrior' *(wadad iyo waranleh).* Religious leaders and teachers *(wadads)* mediate between man and God and between men. They are expected, for an appropriate fee, to dispense blessings and magical potions, to bless livestock, crops, women—and so contribute to their fecundity, and to conduct all religious services, including weddings, funerals and sacrifices (e.g. in rain-making). There are wide variations in their literacy in Arabic and knowledge of the Quran and in the respect which they enjoy. While these skills can be, and are usually, learnt at religious schools—found even among the nomads—Somalis also believe that religious power *(baraka)* capable of performing miracles can be inherited. Thus there are specialist religious clans such as the Ashraf (and its divisions) which, claiming direct descent from the Prophet Mohamed, is credited with miracle-working powers and treated with special reverence. Such religious men are ideally suited to act as mediators in feuds between secular clans.

Similarly, saints are widely believed to possess special powers of blessing in view of their privileged intimacy with the Prophet and through him with God. Regular pilgrimages are made to the tombs of the main saints—some of whom are clan ancestors like Sheikhs Darod and Isaq, and others revered solely for their religious powers as with Sheikh Yusuf Aw Barkhadle (literally 'the Blessed Yusuf') at whose shrine to the west of Hargeisa pilgrims gather from all over the country. He is credited with the introduction of the Arabian black-headed fat-tailed sheep bred locally today, and with inventing a Somali notation for the Arabic vowels which made it easier for Somalis to learn Arabic. People believe that going three times to his tomb in pilgrimage has the same religious value and earns the same blessing as going once on the *haj* to Mecca. This pioneering Muslim missionary who probably came to Somalia in the 12th century is known in the Bay region of southern Somalia as 'Fifty-times Blessed'.

The popular cult of saints, and the belief in the therapeutic powers of charms and amulets employing verses from the Quran, is very important in daily life. One of the commonest remedies is to drink a healing potion made by washing a freshly written Quranic text into a cup. This ingestion of Holy Writ is considered especially effective when written by a pious holy man. Most other magical remedies depend for their effectiveness on their connection with the Quran and other sources of Islamic power. Although popular Somali Islam includes belief in the powers (generally malevolent) of spirits which are especially attracted to women, unlike its position in most African cultures, witchcraft is not a prominent force. Spirit possession illnesses (*saar* or *mingis*) in women which can be treated either by exorcism or by initiation into women's ritual groups are commoner in towns than in rural conditions. Their treatment is costly, and falls most heavily on the male next of kin—husbands, and fathers and brothers in the case of unmarried women. Men sceptically regard these afflictions in their womenfolk as devices which the subordinated sex use against the dominant males.

This sceptical, or at best ambiguous, attitude towards mystical power is characteristic of the Somalis who, while acknowledging that God is the ultimate causal force in the universe, prudently also seek more immediate causes and remedies. There is thus usually no contradiction in employing powerful modern medicines alongside traditional remedies with an Islamic base. Here as in other aspects of their lives, Somalis are staunch pragmatists, valuing what can be shown to produce results. They are quite capable of ridiculing the credulity of those who place an excessive trust in the power of saints or other mystical sources. Indeed, there is a quite well-developed traditional lore in bone-setting and minor surgery, and including the more hazardous trepanning. To say this, of course, is not to suggest that these and such other regularly performed operations as clitoridectomy and infibulation (physical techniques for ensuring virginity before marriage) were carried out with scrupulous attention to hygiene.

Traditional medical lore also included small-pox vaccination and the isolation of patients with diseases which were known to be infectious. In setting this somewhat patchy indigenous heritage in perspective, it should also be remembered, as the explorer Richard Burton recorded in 1855, that Somalis knew that mosquitoes carried malaria before this was discovered by Western science. The success of more recent mass vaccination and innoculation schemes were examples of an application of modern primary health care methodologies. There is thus much to be said for objective reassessment of traditional treatments and therapies and their possible value in conjunction with the introduction of new health provisions—as is the trend elsewhere in the world.

7. The Oral Heritage

Somalis attach great importance to oratory and poetry. It is in these fields, rather than in the plastic arts which are little developed, that Somali culture's most impressive achievements are to be found. This corresponds to the nomadic bias of a people used to travelling light with few material encumbrances—but a richly compensating gift of language. Somalis are born talkers. Every elder is expected to be able to hold an audience for hours on end with a speech richly laced by judicious proverbs and quotations from famous poems and sayings. Similarly, if he is to command respect, he should also be capable not only of composing striking impromptu verse in the various traditional styles, but also of reciting the classic works of famous authors. Since until the mass literacy campaigns of 1972 and 1974 this oral heritage was not preserved in writing, it implied prodigious powers of memory.

This, indeed, is one of the most striking characteristics of Somali nomads whose formidable stores of knowledge makes some elders seem like walking encyclopaedias. Although knowledge is primarily local, Somalis are also keenly interested in world news—which they often interpret somewhat ethnocentrically. They are true radio enthusiasts with an apparently insatiable appetite for broadcasts. Today, as in the time of Seyyid Mohamed Abdille Hassan who owed much of his fame to his oratory and poetry, the spoken word is the key to power and influence amongst the Somali. It is through this medium rather than the visual one that the mass of the population can be effectively reached. Paradoxically, the introduction of written Somali, mainly in towns, quickened Somali nationalist feeling associated with the language. Spoken Somali more than any other single factor provides the 'open sesame' to Somali society and culture. Although fluency in Somali is a powerful precondition, it does not, of course, guarantee acceptance; command of Somali potentially gives access to secrets which may be jealously guarded.

One of the contexts in which men, particularly, are most

relaxed is when they meet socially to chew the leaves of the stimulant plant *qat*. Whereas *qat*-chewing sessions were once special and occassional pastimes, in the 1980s and 1990s the consumption of *qat*, during the day as well as in the evening and individually, became pervasive in urban centres such as Mogadishu.The young militia figures tended to chew it regularly and were provided with supplies by their leaders. Marketing qat became in the 1990s big business and played an important role in the political economy of the 'warlords'.

8. Self-image and National Characteristics

If Somalis are appreciative of the efforts of foreigners to master their language, their pleasure is tinged with deeply ingrained suspicions. Despite their strong sentiments of national self-esteem, they wish to guard the secrets of their culture, and only to share them on their own terms and as they choose.

The suspicion which greets the stranger is not reserved only for non-Somali foreigners. People of one clan behave similarly towards those of another, potentially hostile group. The cautious traditional greeting, 'Is it Peace?', shouted at a distance while approaching, is frequently a literal request for information. In the harsh struggle for survival which is the nomad's lot, suspicion is the natural attitude towards those with whom one competes for access to scarce pastures and water. This defence mechanism is extended to all contexts of social interaction and hence becomes a national characteristic.

Since generosity, especially in receiving guests, is also highly valued and a source of pride, the stranger often encounters conflicting attitudes in his hosts.

This guarded approach to the outside world, coupled with a politician's gift for seizing the advantage, makes the Somalis formidable adversaries. These qualities amongst the nomads are combined with an aggressive self-confidence and, traditionally, open contempt for other people. This is closely bound up with the nomad's sense of independence and defiant scorn for those who seek to impose their dominion upon him. Displays of superior force earn only temporary respect as these most ungovernable people bide their time. The reputation of 'each man his own sultan' suggests that a would-be-leader may argue with them or cajole, but cannot securely command. Connected with this is a certain lack of predictability in routine situations. Particularly outside their traditional nomadic setting, with its inbuilt pattern of impulses and constraints, Somalis are brilliant improvisers and entrepreneurs, if less dependable in humdrum tasks.

These qualities which have so impressed foreigners in their relations with Somalis are somewhat softened amongst the cultivating Digil and Rahanweyn. Here, there is less nonchalant individualism, more respect for authority, a less aggressive welcome, a less suspicious response. This difference in temperament, corresponding to the difference between nomad and farmer, is recognised by both parties and explained in myths which stress the complementary role of both, but the superiority of the nomad.

Part Two: Pre- and Post-Colonial History

9. The Imperial Partition (1880-1941)

Although the Somali people had, traditionally, a strong sense of cultural and linguistic unity, they did not form a single political unit. They were a nation, not a state, although they possessed all the prerequisites for effective statehood. The six major divisions of the nation (the Dir, Isaq, Darod etc.) did not regularly act as stable or autonomous political units. They were too large and widely dispersed to do this, and lacked the necessary organisation. They were in fact themselves divided into a host of subsidiary clans and clan divisions whose members were frequently widely scattered in their nomadic movements. Throughout the entire nation, these divisions were based primarily on tracing kinship in the male line. Groups were formed on the basis of descent traced in this way from common ancestors. Hence family genealogies provided the basis of group division and political identity.

Clans and their lineage divisions were led by 'the elders' in principle all senior adult men. The most stable unit in a flexible and shifting pattern of alignments was the *diya*-paying group'. This consisted usually of a few hundred male heads of closely related families who were parties to a joint treaty or contract (*heer*) to pay and receive compensation for injuries or death or, in default, seek revenge. Some clans had institutionalised clan heads, but in general this was a republican society, without the chiefs found so widely elsewhere in Africa.

These divisions within the otherwise generally homogeneous Somali national culture facilitated the imperial partition of this region during the scramble for Africa. In the closing decades of the 19th century, the two super-powers competing in the region were the British and the French. Their primary interest centred on control of the Nile waters. The British were installed at Aden and sought to prevent or minimise French colonisation on the adjacent Somali coast. They used their allies, the Italians, as an additional means of countering French ambitions. The French had a somewhat similar relationship with the Russians. To safeguard the supply of Somali mutton for the Aden garrison the

British signed 'protection' treaties with a number of northern Somali clans in the 1880s. The French and the Italians did likewise. During the revolt against Anglo-Egyptian rule in the Sudan led by the Sudanese Mahdi, the French, Russians and Italians poured arms into Ethiopia. Russia and Italy were competing to make Ethiopia a client state.

These aspirations were dashed at the battle of Adowa in 1896 when the Ethiopians used their new weapons to rout an Italian army based in the expanding Italian colony of Eritrea. Having already seized the Muslim citadel of Harar in 1884 (visited by the British explorer, Richard Burton,* in 1856), Menelik was now firmly installed as Emperor of Ethiopia and engaged on a policy of imperial expansion and aggrandisement. Britain, France, Russia and Italy were forced to recognise that Ethiopia was the local super-power and had to trim their ambitions accordingly. Russia, at this point, effectively withdrew, leaving arms and some military advisers behind. Britain, France and Italy negotiated with Menelik whose armies were now seeking to impose Ethiopian (i.e. Amhara—the ruling ethnic group) dominion over Cushitic-speaking Oromo and Somali peoples round Harar and to the south-east.

In this process, the Somali nation was divided into five parts. That based on Djibouti which, with the construction of the Franco-Ethiopian railway to Addis Ababa, became Ethiopia's main port, was under French rule and included ethnically related Afar tribesmen. Next came the British Somaliland Protectorate which had Hargeisa as its main town, and its neighbour Italian Somalia, with Mogadishu as its capital. Other Somalis eventually came under the British flag in Northern Kenya. Finally, the fifth division consisted of that large area known after its main Somali residents as the Ogaden, and the Somali territory round Dire Dawa (Dire Dabbe in Somali). This was the Ethiopian portion, although Ethiopian jurisdiction was not at the time unambiguously acknowledged by Britain or Italy. This was partly because recognition of Ethiopian title to the area was in conflict with prior Anglo-Somali treaties and because Italy retained wider

* See his *First Footsteps in East Africa* (1856) 1966.

aspirations. These five divisions of the nation are represented in the five-pointed Somali star, the national emblem adopted by the Somali Republic at the time of independence in 1960.

This division and the encroachment by Christian colonisers provoked a violent reaction. The fiery Ogaden religious leader, Seyyid Mohamed Abdille Hassan and his Dervish forces mounted their protracted guerilla campaign to drive the 'infidel' usurpers out of Somali territory and to regain Somali independence. Significantly, the first major engagement—against the Ethiopians—took place at Jigjiga. Ironically, when in 1920 this 'holy war' finally collapsed and Seyyid Mohamed died, all the colonial powers were more deeply entrenched than before. The British had been forced to assume control of the hinterland, and not merely the coast as they had intended originally, and the Italians were consolidating their colony of Somalia in which they were encouraging Italian settlers to develop fruit plantations.

Friction between the Italians and Ethiopians over the frontier demarcating their respective zones was encouraged by Italy's long term thrust to gain control of Ethiopia and by Ethiopia's own expansionist designs. The conflict was brought to flashpoint by a confrontation in 1935 between the two sides at the oasis of Walwal in the eastern Somali Ogaden. The ensuing fascist conquest of Ethiopia was completed a year later and, in the early phases of World War Two, the Italians drove the British out of their Somali Protectorate, setting up their short lived Italian East African Empire.

10. The Repartition of the Somalis (1941-1960)

After the defeat of the Italians by the Allies in 1941, with the exception of Djibouti, the Somali region came under British military rule. In the subsequent Big Four Power (Britain, France, USA and the USSR) negotiations on the future status of the ex-Italian colonies, Britain originally proposed the formation of a united Somali state under UN Trusteeship and British administration, although British administration was not insisted on. This proposal, however, was rejected, and the Somali nation again partitioned. The British Somaliland Protectorate was reinstated and the Italians returned in 1950 to administer their former colony of Somalia for a period of ten years under UN Trusteeship. The Ogaden and adjacent Somali territories, despite vigorous protests by their inhabitants, were gradually returned to Ethiopian rule. Somali nationalist political parties, encouraged by the benevolent paternalism of British military rule in Somalia from 1941-1950, were now strongly active. The recovery of self-determination in the Somali area of Eastern Ethiopia (Western Somaliland) was already an acute issue.

Ethiopia was thus doubly compensated for the fascist conquest. With Haile Selassie reinstalled on his throne, Ethiopia was given both the Ogaden and neighbouring Somali areas and the former Italian colony of Eritrea. Eritrea was initially federated to Ethiopia in 1952, but a decade later had been annexed as simply another province of Haile Selassie's empire. This action led to the formation of the Eritrean separatist movements and their guerrilla struggle which was to become one of the longest and landmark liberation struggles on the Continent. (Eritrea became independent in 1993.)

11. Independence 1960-1969

Following the desires of the political leaders in both countries, British Somaliland was prepared for independence so that it could join with Somalia when the latter became independent in 1960. In the event, the British Protectorate became self-governing on 26th June, and on 1st July 1960 joined with Italian Somalia to form the Somali Republic under a government formed from those then in power in the two territories. The Prime Minister was Dr Abdirashid Ali Shermarke, who had studied political science in Italy, and the President Adan Abdulle Osman.

The problem of satisfactorily blending the Italian and British colonial traditions was a major preoccupation during the first few years of independence. Apart from the language problem which pervaded all spheres of activity, there were wide divergences between Italian and British practice in administration, bureaucratic procedure, accounting, law etc.

These were not easily resolved and there was often considerable friction between British- and Italian-trained personnel. A typical symptom of this was the abortive northern officers' coup of 1961. By the mid-60s, however, a considerable degree of effective integration had in fact been achieved, both in politics and in administration. The political parties had come to accept the Somali Republic as an established fact and readjusted their alignments correspondingly.

This process was in some respects eased by the majority position enjoyed by the major party, the Somali Youth League (founded in 1943), and by the ties of kinship binding elected members of the National Assembly to their rural constituents. While nationalist leaders sought to eradicate these internal clan divisions within the nation, they continued to exert a pervasive influence on all aspects of life. The persistent power of traditional loyalties leading to the preferment of individuals irrespective of their qualifications made it extremely difficult for the bureaucracy to function efficiently. In a nationalistic atmosphere hostile to those retrograde forces, it became fashionable to refer to clan divisions indirectly rather than directly. In place of their clans people began to speak of their 'ex-clans' and the word 'ex' was adopted into Somali with this sense. Thus, by an adroit trick of language, the problems of clan divisions were ostensibly resolved by consigning them to history and talking about them in the past tense as though they had ceased to exist. This, of course, was not the case.

12. The Pan-Somali Struggle (1960-1969)

While modest developments were being pursued internally with the help of foreign aid, mainly from Western countries, Somali foreign policy was dominated by the Somali unification issue. The Somali Republic founded on Somali national identity was an incomplete state. It did not contain the whole nation, three parts of which remained under foreign rule in Ethiopia, Djibouti and northern Kenya. The main initial thrust here was directed towards Kenya. Prior to Kenyan independence, negotiations with Britain sought to gain autonomy, separate from Kenya, for the northern Somali districts. When, under pressure from Kenya's nationalist leaders, Britain disregarded the report of an official British Commission on Somali aspirations in the area, the Somali Republic broke off diplomatic relations with the United Kingdom. This rebuff caused great resentment amongst the Somali population of northern Kenya and led to the Somali guerrilla campaign (known to the Kenyan authorities as the 'shifta' or bandit war) which paralysed the region from 1963-67.

It was natural to focus the Pan-Somali self-determination issue primarily on the Somali community in northern Kenya in the run-up to Kenyan independence. But it was not possible to ignore Somali aspirations elsewhere. The creation of the Somali Republic inevitably encouraged nationalist sentiment in the Ogaden and incidents between Somali nomads and the Ethiopian military authorities became increasingly frequent. Despite UN and Italian efforts in the period 1950-60 to reach agreement on the definition of the boundary between Somalia and Ethiopia, there was still no generally agreed frontier between the two states. The line shown on the map was still the provisional administrative line used during the British Military Administration of the area.

At the end of 1963 a Somali uprising in the Ogaden led to a brief major confrontation between the Ethiopian and Somalian armed forces. With Pan-Somali nationalism exerting such influence and with American and Western military support for Ethiopia and Kenya, it was natural that the Somali Republic should reject an offer of limited defensive arms from the West in favour of a more generous and open-ended Soviet arms commitment. This Russian military connexion which did not at the time lead Somalia to move far from her neutralist but generally pro-Western stance, was to have far-reaching effects later.

The new civilian government formed in June 1967 under the Premiership of Mohamed Haji Ibrahim Egal, a northerner from the ex-British Protectorate, and with Abdirashid Ali Shermarke as President, led to a marked shift in Somali foreign policy. Concluding that the aggressive pursuit of the Pan-Somali struggle favoured by previous governments had yielded little positive return, Premier Egal embarked on a policy of detente with Kenya and Ethiopia, seeking to gain a new understanding with the leaders of both countries as a basis for more fruitful negotiation.

This development, which thrust the Pan-Somali issue temporarily into the background, was one of many factors which contributed to the eventual downfall of Premier Egal and his replacement by military rule. What turned out to be Somalia's last elections were held in March 1969, when 1,002 candidates representing 62 parties (mainly thinly disguised clan organisations) competed for the 123 seats in the National Assembly. The Somali Youth League victory turned into a landslide when all the 'independent' members of the Assembly, with one exception, joined the government party, led by Egal and President Abdirashid. In the usual one-party style, Somalia now came under increasingly autocratic rule, with Egal's government paying little attention to the dissent provoked by its growing autocracy. The assassination of the President on 15 October 1969 administered a sharp jolt and was followed on 21 October by a well-staged military coup in which the army calmly seized power without encountering opposition.

13. Military Rule and Revolution (1969-1974)

The original impetus for the coup came from a group of young army officers impatient with the corruption, nepotism and inefficiency of Egal's government. But it soon became clear that the new Head of State and President of the Supreme Revolutionary Council (SRC), General Mohamed Siyad Barre, Commander of the Amy, held the reins of power firmly in his hands. General Siyad who, like his personal rival the former police commander, General Mohamed Abshir (now placed in detention) had been a police inspector during the British Military Administration, had also trained in Italy where he had privately studied politics. Assisted by a council of largely civilian, technocrat-style, secretaries of state, the SRC—with its 25 members drawn from the army and police, and ranging in rank from general to captain—embarked on an energetic policy of internal administrative reform. The aim, which was popular initially, was to clean out the Augean stables, and restore Somali virtues with a concerted onslaught, under energetic leadership on the real enemies of progress: poverty, disease and ignorance.

Reform and galvanisation of the nation's energies were pursued by a battery of new measures. Civilian district and provincial governors were replaced by military personnel who were installed as chairmen of local revolutionary councils modelled on that in Mogadishu. Unemployed urban tribal drop-outs were recruited for a whole series of public work projects. The death sentence was reintroduced to replace blood compensation (*diya*) paid traditionally in inter-clan feuds. This was part of a wider strategy aimed at abolishing traditional clan divisions.

14. Scientific Socialism in Somalia

These policies acquired a more distinctive ideological edge with the official adoption of Scientific Socialism (in Somali, literally 'wealth-sharing based on knowledge') on the first anniversary of the *coup* in October 1970. The coup had now become retrospectively a 'bloodless revolution'. This change of direction reflected the Army's growing dependence on Russia and the idealistic orientation of young intellectuals unimpressed by Somalia's previous pro-Western policies. This development was coupled with national campaigns and 'crash programmes' against corruption and tribalism, effigies representing those anachronistic 'impediments to progress' being burnt at official ceremonies early in 1971. The word *jaalle*—literally comrade, or friend—was officially launched as the approved term of greeting and address to replace the traditional terms 'uncle' and 'cousin', with their unacceptable clan allusions. Locally-based people's vigilantes were organised to lead community development projects, frequently recruiting from the unemployed. Destitute children and orphan street boys were gathered into Revolutionary Youth Centres where they were clothed, fed and educated in the new revolutionary ideals. At a national level, the same values were instilled along with military training, at the former military academy in Mogadishu, renamed 'Halane' after a Somali lieutenant who had died in the 1964 Somali-Ethiopian fighting while attempting to save his country's colours.

At the same time, under the diligent direction of the Ministry of Information and National Guidance, a national cult, amalgamating Chinese, North Korean and Nasserite as well as Soviet influence, was created round the Head of State as benevolent 'Father' of a nation whose 'Mother' was the 'Glorious Revolution'. This cult of the President was accompanied by the publication of pithy extracts from his speeches and sayings (e.g. 'less talk and more work') and in radio programmes which ingeniously blended these and Marxist themes with Islamic motifs. The political office of the Presidency was expanded into a national organisation of *apparatchiks* staffing local orientation centres, established in all main settlements. The walls of these, in common with public posters, featured the new ruling trinity of *Jaalle* Markis (Marx), *Jaalle* Lenin and *Jaalle* Siyad. Revolutionary vigilance was maintained by the National Security Service (NSS), with arbitrary powers of arrest and detention, and the National Security Courts which, dispensing with legal safeguards on individual liberty, dealt out a rough justice. In a further effort to reduce the continuing influence of clan ties—acknowledged in a number of the President's bitter harangues—the eight* provinces of the Republic were reconstituted as fifteen new regions, comprising seventy-eight districts, renamed where necessary to exclude clan names, e.g. Mijerteinia became Bari. Stress was placed on the settlement as a basic unit of identification in place of clan allegiance, and marriages, traditionally inter-clan affairs, were celebrated in Orientation Centres and stripped of clan significance. In the same spirit, the former lineage and clan heads (chiefs and elders) were re-named 'peace-seekers' and theoretically transformed into part of the state bureaucracy.

This assault on the traditional structure of society in an effort to secure modernisation was coupled with a policy of state control of the economy. The export of the banana crop grown in the riverine areas south of Mogadishu was controlled by a state

---

* Up to this time, the phrase 'ninth region' was used jocularly as a euphemism to refer to prison or banishment on courses' in the USSR.

TABLE 1

DADKA IYO DUUMYADA DALKA KU DHAQHAYD GOBOLLADA 1975

SOMALIA'S POPULATION BY REGIONS 1975

GOBOL REGION	DADKA / POPULATION			XOOLAHA / LIVESTOCK			
	Lab Male	Dheddig Female	Dhammaan Total	Geel Camel	Lo' Cattle	Ido Sheep	Riyo Goats
W.Galbeed	228,418	211,415	439,833	606,224	145,154	2,241,685	3,076,087
Togdheer	136,814	120,957	257,771	320,432	43,554	917,490	902,387
Sanaag	71,843	73,565	145,408	205,214	74,451	1,521,386	664,278
Bari	81,669	72,683	154,352	240,214	14,918	1,387,678	2,094,802
Nugaal	42,906	42,234	85,140	154,734	12,386	223,411	611,296
Mudug	114,722	100,420	215,142	751,458	340,472	1,135,977	2,744,372
Galguduud	93,898	87,757	181,655	395,455	217,826	587,875	1,734,322
Hiiraan	76,043	71,238	147,281	460,521	169,695	287,392	1,159,372
Sh.Dhexe	123,537	112,862	236,399	236,066	365,683	324,831	720,318
Muqdisho	188,676	181,995	370,671	910	21,927	5,634	18,655
Sh.Hoose	203,917	194,169	398,086	292,730	418,911	89,521	200,000
J.Hoose	130,202	115,824	246,026	296,615	1,036,155	81,477	177,372
Gedo	112,019	100,072	212,091	784,283	527,696	500,095	724,888
Bay	157,104	144,950	302,054	361,619	254,877	54,626	191,999
Bakool	53,722	46,375	100,097	191,674	100,373	79,008	274,065
DHAMMAAN TOTAL	1,815,490	1,676,516	3,492,006	5,297,239	3,722,151	9,432,320	15,275,558

agency not greatly different from the monopoly established by previous civilian governments. Similarly, grain production was controlled, farmers being allowed to keep a small quantity of grain for their own use, and obliged to sell the rest at fixed prices to the Agricultural Development Corporation which stored it and arranged for its distribution and sale to the public. Imported goods were similarly regulated through a state agency. The major local industry, the sugar factory at Jowhar, and the meat processing plant at Kismayu, were likewise state enterprises. This impressive apparatus of state machinery was, however, only part of the picture. The mainstay of the country's economy remained the pastoral sector from which livestock, Somalia's main product, were exported on the hoof to the Arab markets by private enterprise, although hides and skins were mainly exported via a government agency. Private import/export companies and construction firms continued to pursue a lucrative trade, and, on a smaller scale, small urban businesses and shops followed these old patterns of free enterprise, sometimes under new labels.

The Supreme Revolutionary Council's revolutionary aims were most directly pursued through national 'crash programmes' launched by the President with full military honours. The most impressive of these were undoubtedly the urban and rural mass literacy campaigns of 1973 and 1974. Previous civilian governments had never had the courage to decide on and implement a script for the national language. The issue was indeed controversial with public opinion divided between supporters of Arabic, the Latin script, and various Somali-invented scripts. President Siyad's regime sensibly adopted the Latin script, which was the most suitable medium, and proceeded to encourage mass literacy. In the 1973 urban campaign, officials were given intensive courses which they had to pass at reasonable levels if they wished to retain their positions. Voluntary adult literacy classes proved popular and successful.

The following year, the scheme, enlarged to include health and veterinary components, was extended to the rural and largely nomadic population through a nation-wide Campaign for

Rural Development, employing some 30,000 secondary school students and their teachers. Unfortunately, this programme turned out to coincide with one of the worst droughts in Somali history, in which a quarter of a million nomads lost most of their livestock and had to be supported in relief camps and later grouped in agricultural and fishing settlements, mainly in southern Somalia. In this humane response to a national calamity, the government seized the opportunity of promoting its long-term aim of curtailing nomadism and of inculcating the new revolutionary ideals among the refractory nomadic population.

15. The Resumption of the Pan-Somali Struggle (1974-1978)

The first phase of General Siyad's rule (1969-1974) was one of concentration on internal problems: local development and consolidation of the regime's authority. 1974 marked the inauguration of a new expansive phase. In that year Somalia joined the Arab League, thereby gaining some leverage with Russia, and also hosted and chaired the Organisation of African Unity Heads of State meeting. This new prominence invited a more thrusting policy on the pan-Somali issue, to which added piquancy was inevitably given by the increasing paralysis of Ethiopia in the wake of Haile Selassie's overthrow in September 1974. Somalia's military rulers had introduced the customary anti-imperialist rhetoric (refreshingly unstressed in Somalia prior to 1969) and this was now mainly directed towards France in relation to Djibouti and Ethiopia. African support here was, naturally, mainly restricted to the Djibouti self-determination issue. Especially because of the sensitivity of African frontiers, it was difficult for African governments to rally to Somalia's side in its denunciation of Ethiopian imperialism which, being black, hardly counted. The pace of events in Djibouti progressed with surprising speed, reaching a somewhat unexpected conclusion in June 1977 when the territory became independent under a Somali President. Without going into details, the territory had swung from Afar domination back to an uneasy Somali-Afar alliance, under Somali leadership, bolstered up by French and

Arab support. This outcome was something for which the architects of Somalia's external policies could take some credit.

The Somali government was now, however, under very heavy pressure from its co-nationals and their allies in Ethiopia. In the wake of the early Ogaden insurgency of 1960-1964 a similar, but more recalcitrant guerrilla movement had arisen among the Muslim (Arussi) Oromo in Bale Province. Having finally made peace with Haile Selassie in 1970 and received a traditional Ethiopian title, the leader of this rising, Wako Guto, followed many of his kinsmen in seeking asylum in Somalia. These and other anti-Amhara dissidents from the Ogaden were constantly pressing the Somali government to come to their aid in a concerted liberation struggle against their Ethiopian rulers. The Ogaden nationalists had already set up their widely appealing Western Somali Liberation Front (WSLF), which was allied to the Bale insurgents who became active again in 1975-6. By the spring of 1977, Oromo guerrilla forces had recovered control of most of the countryside in Bale and in the north the war in Eritrea had reached a critical phase, with the local nationalists controlling most of the region and pressing heavily on the beleaguered and demoralised Ethiopian garrisons in Asmara and Massawa.

As the new military leaders in Ethiopia increasingly proclaimed their dedication to revolutionary socialism, the urgency of finding a solution for Somali nationalism in Eastern Ethiopia (or 'Western Somalia') was reflected in a Russo-Cuban venture which brought Fidel Castro to the region in March 1977 to mediate between Colonel Mengistu and General Siyad. This underlined the Russian interest in Ethiopia, which increased as Ethiopia's relations with her traditional patrons, the USA, deteriorated, partly as a consequence of the Carter administration's reluctance to continue to supply arms which would be applied to suppress the Eritrean nationalists. (America had, of course, acquired Diego Garcia and could, presumably, afford to dispense with the older strategic installation base at Kagnew in Eritrea).

Mengistu's visit to Moscow in May seemed to set the seal on the seismic shift of super-power allegiances in the area and was the final precipitant leading to the war in Eastern Ethiopia/Western

Somalia. The Western Somali Liberation Front, or their allies, began their military campaign to expel the Ethiopians from Somali ethnic territory by cutting the strategically significant line of rail between Addis and Djibouti on the eve of the latter's independence. With tacit and cautious support from the SDR, the Western Somali Liberation Front launched the whirlwind advance which, by late September 1977, brought its forces to the gates of Harar in the wake of the retreat by the demoralised Ethiopian forces. Russia now rallied to Ethiopia's defence mounting a massive airlift of sophisticated military equipment with Russian and East German military advisers, and Cuban and South Yemeni combat troops. Inevitably Somali-Soviet relations rapidly deteriorated. The anticipated breach occurred on 13 Novenber less than a month after the successful rescue of the hijacked Lufthansa jet at Mogadishu airport which opened the door to an unprecedented influx of Western aid.

The Russian exodus from Somalia and the victories in the Ogaden led to immense elation, and greatly increased the popularity of the Siyad regime. The terrible debacle which followed in the spring of 1978 when, with Russo-Cuban support and greatly superior firepower, the Ethiopians reimposed their rule in Western Somalia, inevitably shook the Somali government to its foundations.

Although the Somalis had understood the United States to have indicated its willingness to replace Russia as Somalia's patron superpower, this had not actually happened. For the time being, because of the sensitivity of the question of the frontiers of African states, American and indeed Western aid generally seemed restricted to civilian projects. This left a yawning gulf, exacerbating internal sources of instability—all greatly increased since the Ogaden War and its outcome. The most obvious manifestation of the delicacy of the political situation in Somalia was the abortive military coup of April 1978, which far from 'clearing the air' in the Republic, left things as confused and uncertain as ever. The regime's survival, though by no means assured, was, in the short term at least, encouraged by the divisions among those who opposed it.

16. The Russian Legacy

The enthusiasm with which the public greeted the Russian departure in part reflected the way in which the Russians were generally identified with the more oppressive aspects of the Siyad government, particularly, the National Security Service and the National Security Courts. In the summer of 1978 there was some evidence that, without their Russian and East German advisers, those organisations were considered to be less arbitrary in their activities and less threatening to ordinary people. Whether or not this reflected also a deliberate policy decision at the centre of power, or a weakening of the centre's hold (suggested by other factors) was hard to assess.

Those who wished to, could find some support for the former interpretation in the announcement on the 9th anniversary of the Revolution in October 1978 that there would be a constitution and a return to parliamentary rule. It was announced that some 3,000 prisoners (presumably some held for political reasons) would be released. A few days later, the seventeen people who had been found guilty of leading the April coup were publicly executed by firing squad.

The Constitution and 'people's parliament' established in 1979 in the spirit of 'democratic centralism' would clearly provide new scope for the official Somali Revolutionary Socialist Party formed, under Soviet pressure, in June 1976. This organisation with an official membership of just over 12,000 in 1977,[*] the majority classed as 'workers and employees' and 735 as 'peasants', was a direct outgrowth of the earlier Political Office of the Presidency which it replaced. The Party was directed by a Supreme Council with 73 members, one a woman. The Central Committee of the Party, incorporating members of the former Supreme Revolutionary Council was divided into 19 departments, each headed by a Committee member, and linked with the various Government ministries and state agencies. All government ministers, with the exception of the Transport Min-

* Ref. 'Party Life', in *Halgan*, July 1977, pp. 9-33.

ister, were members of the Central Committee. The vital Political Bureau, the real seat of authority and power, was led by the President of the Republic and Chairman of the Party, General Siyad, aided by the three Vice-Presidents (Minister of Defence; Assistant to President for Presidential Affairs; and Assistant to the Chairman for Party Affairs) and by the Head of the National Security Service.

If these developments appeared to provide a more representative government in which the younger civilian intellectuals had a more formalised position, there was no question as to the ultimate source of power. Indeed, in the wake of the Ogaden defeat and the rupture with Russia it appeared, as might have been anticipated, that the President was consolidating his position on traditionalist lines. Despite all the rhetoric directed against tribalism and clan ties, members of the public tended to regard President Siyad's regime as based primarily on three main traditional division of the Darod clan confederacy. These were his own clan, the Marrehan, based on the middle Juba; his mother's clan, the Ogaden; and that of his son-in-law and head of the National Security Service, the Dulbahante. The last-named straddled the border between the former British Somaliland Protectorate and Italian Somalia and hence acted as a highly significant lynchpin in the structure of the united Republic.

This configuration of family ties summed up in the clandestine nick-name 'MOD' proved a powerful formula for rule in the Somali Democratic Republic. In practice what was implied was that, in relation to their numbers, these three groups were over-represented in key positions throughout the state. Otherwise, as can be seen from the table, comparing the composition of successive Somali governments, General Siyad's regime contained members of all the major clan groups on the established, if disavowed principle of clan representation.

TABLE 2

Composition of Somali Governments[*] by major lineage blocs, 1960-1975

	1960[1]	1964[2]	1967[3]	1969[4]	1975[5]
Darod	6	6	6	6	10
Digil and Rahanweyn	2	3	3	2	0
Dir	0	1	1	0	2
Hawiye	4	3	4	5	4
Isaq	2	3	4	5	4
	14	16	18	18	20

1. The first administration of Somalia formed after independence in 1960, headed by Premier Abdi Rashid Ali Shermarke (Darod). The President and non-executive Head of State was Adan Abdulle Osman (Hawiye).

2. Government formed under the leadership of Abdirazak Haji Husseyn (Darod), Adan Abdulle Osman remaining President of the Republic.

3. Government formed by Mohamed Haji Ibrahim Egal (Isaq) from the northern (ex-British) regions of the Republic. Dr. Abdi Rashid Ali Shermarke(Darod) had now become President.

4. Second government formed by Mohamed Haji Ibrahim Egal following March 1969 elections, Dr. Abdi Rashid Ali Shermarke remaining President.

5. Supreme Revolutionary Council, as of 1975, following various changes in composition since the military *coup* of October 1969. The Council was officially dissolved in July 1976 with the formation of the Somali Socialist Revolutionary Party. This had a Central Committee of 73 members and a Politburo of five, (including the three SRC Vice-Presidents and the Head of the National Security Service) presided over by the Head of State and Party Secretary-General, General Mohamed Siyad Barre.

* Cabinet Ministers only are included here and, after 1969, members of the Supreme Revolutionary Council. The Somali nation as a whole comprises the five major lineage blocs (or 'clan families' as I have called them in previous publications: see Lewis, 1961), whose representation in successive Somali governments is shown in the table.

The regime's power-base was significantly widened by the opening of the 'people's parliament', with 171 elected members (all belonging to the SRS Party) at the end of December 1979. President Siyad reshuffled his cabinet and abolished the titles, if not the roles, of his three Vice-presidents. With the refugee crisis (see below) obviously aggravated by lack of fuel supplies, in October 1980, the President felt it necessary to declare a state of emergency and resurrected the Supreme Revolutionary Council. He thus sought to regain firm control of an increasingly difficult situation and to combat corruption and inefficiency. Confronted by mounting insecurity—internally and externally—it was natural that the regime should attempt to retrench itself with all the means at its disposal. These included the formal power structure developed in the first years of the Revolution and the more traditional clan ties referred to above.

Thus as nationalism and Islam counted for far more than ideology in foreign policy, so at home traditional forces continued to play a decisive role in politics, whatever the official picture. The latter, after the breach with Russia, continued to stress dedication to Socialism, with perhaps less emphasis on the qualifying adjective 'scientific'. Cynical Somali commentators observed that the Socialist path provided a convenient formula for autocracy. It seemed likely, however, that there might be an abatement of the tension between Socialism and traditionalist Islam of which the most violent instance was the execution in January 1975 of ten religious leaders who had attacked liberal new measures designed to give women equal inheritance rights to men.

17. Government and Rural Society

The governmental reorganisation associated with the establishment of the Party had significant implications for the administration of the country as a whole. The Ministry of the Interior which had formerly controlled the Police Force was disbanded, its functions being parcelled out between the Presidency, the Party, the Ministry of Local Government and Rural Development, and such state agencies as the Resettlement

Agency, Cooperatives Board, and the Agricultural Crash Programme. Just as formerly the Central SRC structure had been replicated at Regional and District level by corresponding local Councils, so now the regional and district administrative units came under the authority of corresponding Party Committees. Thus the role of Regional Governor merged with that of Regional Party Secretary, and District Governor merged with District Secretary, the resulting key official being aided by a First Assistant for Party Affairs and a Second Assistant for Administrative Affairs. The appointment and operation of these local administrative officials was overseen and coordinated by a Regional Inspectorate of high-ranking officials (several of them military officers) reporting to the President, formally via the Vice-President and Presidential Affairs Assistant, General Husseyn Kulmiye, (a former Minister of the Interior). Despite these elaborate changes in nomenclature, there was much continuity between the 1980s regional power structure and the earlier organisation based on Revolutionary Councils. Regional and district governors were still closely controlled by the Presidency. Their actions being subject to the vigilant scrutiny of the local heads of the National Security Service (NSS), and buttressed by the local police and army commanders. While some Regional and District headquarters could muster small associations of workers with whom to discuss local issues, the main linkage between this official state apparatus and the bulk of the rural population was through the local elders. These established traditional figures had been officially known since the Revolution as 'Peace Seekers' (*Nabad-doon*) and would act as intermediaries between their clansmen and the official authorities. Local religious leaders (sheikhs—in Somali *wadaad*) played a similar consultative role.

Part Three: Society and Economy

18. Traditional Rural Social Institutions

The most pervasive organisational principle in traditional Somali social organisation is kinship, traced patrilineally in the male line. Genealogies tracing descent (*tol*) from common ancestors are the basis for the division of the population into clan and sub-clan. Despite the effect of the increasing monetarisation of the traditional economy, of official measures designed to eradicate clan loyalties, and other forces for change, these ties continue to provide the individual's primary identity within the Somali nation. The kinship unit with which the individual identifies himself is always relative and varies according to the situation in which allegiance is evoked. For instance, people of Darod descent so identify themselves in opposition to Isaq, Hawiye, Dir, Digil and Rahanweyn. Within Darod, the further divisions of Ogaden, Mijerteyn, Marrehan, Dulbahante and other clans become relevant. Each of these clans comprise hundreds of subdivisions which, in turn, act on occasion as separate opposed groups. These kinship ties are in fact traced backwards through the individual's father, his father's father, the latter's father and so on until the founding ancestor, (Darod, Isaq, etc.) is reached. The 'number of generations counted apart', as Somali put it, provide a ready-reckoner of closeness or remoteness in people's relations with each other. The term 'cousin' (or in the case of a younger man addressing an older man, 'uncle') is applied to all those other than brothers who share recognised common descent. The word 'cousin' or 'uncle' is also applied as a polite term of address when speaking to an unrelated stranger. The term *jaalle*, friend, or comrade, introduced by the Siyad regime, sought to replace this traditional usage and its associated and potentially divisive kinship connotations.

Ties with the mother's brother's clan (e.g., those between President Siyad's Marrehan and the Ogaden) are also extremely important. They have a warm, friendly character, and may be used to supplement the axiomatic solidarity based on patrilineal kinship (*tol*). The mother's brother's group is known as *Reer Abti*, *'reer'* being the most general term for 'group' or 'people'. Ties established by marriage (*hidid*) are also significant, especially where as is generally the case amongst the northern Somali nomads, marriage is an alliance contracted between potentially hostile groups.

If patrilineal kinship is the primary bond, it creates diffuse loyalties which are given specific focus by a contractual treaty (heer) defining the limits of solidarity in blood vengeance. The payment and receipt of blood compensation (*diya* in Arabic, *mag* in Somali)—or, in the case of default the duty to pursue vengeance—falls on a restricted group of closely related kin who accept this as a collective obligation. Such compensation agreements detailing the way in which a particular group of kin would protect the life and property of their members were, during the colonial period, lodged in District Office headquarters, and *diya*-paying groups formed on this basis behaved and were treated as the primary political divisions of the population. Although official policy after independence, and especially after the 1969 Revolution, sought to undermine these traditional arrangements, they still persisted in a less formalised fashion. Death by firing squad as the penalty for apprehended murderers during the 'revolutionary' period appeared to result in traditional feud being less common than it once was. However, it was not eradicated, and collective claims for blood compensation were still advanced even in such contexts as urban traffic accidents, with blood-money even said to have been paid out by an insurance company. It was very much in terms of these traditional patterns of clan vengeance that people in the summer of 1978 were discussing the execution of the mainly Mijerteyn leaders of the abortive April coup. This was seen by many as a feud between the Mijerteyn and the President's Marrehan clan, a view which some commentators considered enabled the President to distract attention from wider discontents shared by members of other clans.

At all levels of grouping, policy is traditionally decided by the elders (*odayaal*,* singular *oday*—the word *duk* is also used). Some clans have, also, dynastic families of clan heads, some-

* *akhyar* in southern Somalia

times called 'Sultans' (also known as *Ugaas, Garaad, Bogor* etc.), a role which is, on the whole, more defined amongst the southern cultivating Digil and Rahanweyn Somali, living between the Shebelle and Juba Rivers. These southern farming Somali have traditionally had leaders with a more authoritative position than is generally the case among the pastoral nomads. Before they were all re-named 'peace-seekers' (*nabad-doon*) by the revolution-period government, the Digil and Rahanweyn clan leaders were usually known by the colloquial Italian-Arabic title '*Capo-qabila*' (the Arabic word *qabila*, is sometimes applied in Somali to clans)

19. Local Groups and Settlement Patterns

As is to be expected, the pastoral nomads who make up the bulk of the population have a much more fluid and flexible pattern of distribution than the cultivators. The units here called 'clans' (such as Dulbahante, Habar Toljaalo, Marrehan etc.) had and continue to have loosely defined areas of movement. Their most clearly defined bases are the dry season wells customarily used for watering camels when water is scarce. It is usually at such watering places that market and administrative centres have grown up. While amongst the northern nomads at this level of grouping there are roughly established 'spheres of influence', there are also many areas in which different groups regularly graze their stock, and rhythmic seasonal patterns of move-ment—according to the distribution of rain, pasturage and water. So, for example, although the Ogaden region is primarily inhabited by pastoral nomads of the Ogaden clan, there is also seasonal movement in and out of the region by Isaq clans to the north—in the centre of the northern part of the Republic. Rain and the grass it produces is the ultimate determinant of move-ment, other factors (including government intervention) being contingent variables. If rain is evenly distributed in either or both the two main rainy seasons, spring and autumn, the population will be similarly distributed. If, on the contrary, it falls unevenly, there will be corresponding concentrations of pas-toralists. In time of extreme drought, unprecedented nomadic movements in search of grazing take place. Thus in the appalling 1974-1975 drought, famine-stricken nomads from the north drove their few surviving camels over 1000 miles to the hinterland of Mogadishu in search of pasture (for more normal patterns of northern nomadic movement see Hunt 1951 and Lewis 1961).

There are two main types of grazing camp, following the division in herding practices associated with sheep and goat (collectively called *adi*) on the one hand, and camels on the other. Cattle, if they are owned (as is the case in the northwest and southern Somalia), may form a third herding unit but one whose movements are frequently closely associated with those of sheep and goats, since frequency of their watering needs is similar to sheep and goats. A married man moves with his wife and young family with sheep and goats, a few milch camels, and burden camels to transport the collapsible nomad's tent (*aqal*) from place to place. This domestic unit is known as *guri*, from the verb *gur*, to move. Related families tend to move and camp together—although they also often split up into new combinations. Grazing encampments (singular *degmo* from the verb *deg*, to settle) form wherever pasture and water conditions are suitable. Such settlements often consist of 30 or so nuclear or extended families, each camped separately within its own thorn-fence pen, and occupying an area of approximately 20 square miles with a population density of some 20 persons per square mile. Depending on weather conditions, inter-clan relations, government intervention etc., such temporary encampments may only stay in one place for a few weeks and are likely to be separated by large tracts of unoccupied land.

A trend begun in the nineteen sixties in the Togdheer region has been towards more permanent settlement based around cement-lined water tanks (singular, barkad) owned by individual families. Whilst water collected in these reservoirs can hardly be withheld from close kin, excess water from the '*barkads*' would be sold at great profit in dry areas to which it was transported by truck by enterprising traders. This 'premature settlement', as it has been called, led to much heavier grazing around these new water points causing widespread erosion and may have locally exacerbated the effects of the 1974-1975 drought.

Following the drought, a Central Rangelands Development Project was established, funded by the World Bank, which sought to improve the deplorable situation. It combined the balanced provision of water resources with grazing reserves and grazing control. Over the years, increasing population pressure had led to increasingly reckless patterns of livestock overbreeding with short-term survival as the primary goal. There was little support among nomads for government efforts to introduce grazing reserves despite the urgent need for a more rational use of their scarce grazing resources.

The grazing camel units (the *geel her* as they are called) are in the charge of unmarried men and boys who, from the age of about seven, are sent out to learn the demanding skills of Somali pastoral nomadism. Girls stay with the domestic unit based on sheep and goats, helping their mothers care for these smaller stock and performing other domestic tasks such as grinding grain into flour, cooking, and caring for younger siblings. Men are primarily associated with camels—traditionally the most prized Somali possession and standard of wealth. Men milk camels and cope with the burdensome task of loading and unloading transport camels, though it is women who assemble and dismantle the nomadic tent. The camels of closely related kin are herded together and congregate in camel camps in an area of suitable pasture. Each camp is a tightly integrated unit. The camel boys, whose diet is chiefly camel's milk augmented occasionally by a slaughtered animal, sleep together at night on a bed of grass in the centre of the kraal. These camel-herdsmen are thus known as 'those who share the same mat' *(ardaa wadaag)*. Like their counterparts (the domestic family units with the sheep and goats), a group of camel-camps in an area of grazing has little if any sense of residential solidarity and no fixed composition. However, the tendency of camel-herders of the same lineage to cluster together in an area of pasturage is especially pronounced in time of inter-clan hostilities.

These two units—the domestic sheep and goat herding group and the grazing camel unit—are normally most widely separated geographically during the dry seasons when the sheep and goats, which require almost daily watering, have to stay close to the wells while the camels, which can go without water for at least fourteen days, will pasture in remote grazing areas.

In the summer, especially after the spring Gu seasons rains, the two stock units, whose water and pasturage needs can then be satisfied in close proximity, move closer together. This pattern of dry season dispersal and wet season concentration has important social consequences. In the dry season, preoccupation with the survival of herds and humans is acute. In the wet season there is normally abundant milk, livestock most frequently calve after the rains, and a general expansion of social life takes place. In the dry seasons each family head concentrates on coordinating the watering arrangements of his sheep and goats and his far-flung grazing camels. Pressure on resources is heavy and likely to trigger off quarrels over the order of precedence at wells which quickly develop into violent lineage clashes and the revival of rankling lineage feuds. The main wet season, in contrast, brings the young herdsmen and marriageable girls together and is the dating and mating season. It is also the time for other communal rituals, lineage council meetings, and general activity in which there is abundant scope for the oratory and poetising on which the Somalis lay such store. This seasonal division between the negative and positive poles of the year is neatly summed up in the proverb: 'war and drought; peace and plenty' *(ol iyo abaar; nabad iyo 'aano*)*.

Since rarely more than half a flock is likely to be in milk at the same time, and at the end of the dry season only a much smaller fraction, a family of a wife and a few young children require a minimum of 50-60 sheep and goats for survival. The minimum camel (or cattle) requirement is similarly 10-15 milch animals. Depending on the family's own labour supply, a flock of 200 or more sheep and goats, say, require additional help from female relatives. The constant stress on increasing herd size reflects the seasonal uncertainties and the allowance which has to be made for wastage due to drought and disease in this capriciously harsh

* *'aano* literally means 'milk'

environment. Since it is not uncommon for an individual herder to possess over 100 camels worth up to £10,000 (1980s values) it is scarcely realistic to regard all Somali nomads as destitute pastoralists unable to fend for themselves. The problem, however, is that in this uncertain environment a man's riches may disappear almost overnight in the wake of some natural calamity. Thus the Somali nomad is by temperament and practice a gambler who appreciates the transitory nature of success and failure.

20. Livestock Trade and Labour Migration

It cannot be emphasised too strongly that the pastoral nomadism constitutes the economic base of the vast bulk of the Somali population, and manifestations of the nomadic life-style and traditions pervade almost all aspects of Somali life. In contrast to nomadic minorities in other countries, Somalia's nomads are not cut off from the life of urban centres or culturally and socially separated from the majority of urban residents, civil servants and other government employees (e.g. the armed forces). From the President downwards, at all levels of government and administration, those living with a modern life style in urban conditions have brothers and cousins living as nomads in the interior and regularly have shares in joint livestock herds. Civil servants regularly invest in livestock, including camels, which are herded by their nomadic kinsmen.

It is equally important to stress that the nomads have been for centuries part of a vast, monetised, trading network connecting Ethiopia and the Arabian Peninsula. Commercial attitudes are consequently strongly developed. Thus, the pastoral nomads have long maintained a distinction between disposable wealth (*mod* in Somali)—such as cash—and capital, particularly livestock and above all camels (*mal* in Somali). They have sold livestock and livestock products—hides, skins and clarified butterfat—for centuries.

Sales patterns, however, are influenced by local factors and preferences. Traditionally hides and skins are sold in largest quantities in the dry season when sheep and goats are slaughtered for food. Camels and cattle which are traditional stores of wealth (capital assets used as marriage payments, blood money etc.) may not be so readily sold when they are in prime condition in the wet seasons if cash needs can be satisfactorily met by 'target sales' of less highly valued sheep and goats. Camels, which are the hardiest and most prized wealth are least readily sold, except by those who can afford to do so, or are forced to in order to survive. Hides and skins are sold mainly, but not exclusively, through government channels. Stock on the hoof, on the other hand, are purchased by private merchants for export (mainly) to the Gulf States. The pastoralist seller regularly accompanies the buyer to the port of embarkation, or other main transit centre, and only parts with his stock when he receives a cash payment. Merchants who default on payments to pastoralists are liable to summary imprisonment and may also forfeit their reputation and trade. Brokers (dilaal) play an important role in this enterprise using kinship ties as a source of trust and confidence.

It is difficult to generalise about sales patterns since these vary so widely in response to the factors indicated. However, some indications can be given. From a flock of 100 sheep and goats it would not be unusual to cull 30 head for sale (mainly sheep). From a herd of 100 cattle, 10 might be sold, while from a camel herd of the same size only 5 sold, or killed for consumption.

Northern Somalis have a long tradition of labour migration and overseas employment, traditionally mainly crewing on ships. In the decades following independence, the disparity between local wages in Somalia (higher in the north than south), and those obtainable in Arabia and the Gulf States led to a large exodus of able-bodied men. This 'muscle-drain' augments the 'brain-drain' to the same countries, and was especially strong in the two decades from the mid-sixties to mid-eighties, and led to a large influx of remittance earnings in cash and kind. This inflow to dependents and kin, with other factors, led to a marked inflation of prices which were substantially higher in the north than in the south of the country. The ubiquitous transistor radio, so popular amongst the media-conscious nomads with their powerful oral culture and insatiable appetite for radio, became widely disseminated as part of this influx of goods from kinsmen working overseas. This was only one of the more tangible signs of the extent to which the northern pastoral nomads became part of a remittance economy.

21. Northern Cultivating Settlements

In the area of relatively favourable rainfall to the west of Hargeisa in the north where nomads have turned to cultivation over the last hundred years, there is quite a close association between kinship and land holding. This is the result of the direct settlement of pastoral nomads in this region, where the original 'demonstration effect' was provided by local religious settlements and the adjacent cultivating Oromo (Akishu etc.) of the Jigjiga-Harar area. In this region cultivation, mainly of sorghum and Indian corn, is by ox-drawn plough in much the same style as highland Ethiopian farming. Over the last fifteen years or so new innovations involve the substitution of oxen in ploughing by camels and, on large farms, by tractors.

Villages here, consisting of the houses of related families grouped together within a common thorn fence, may contain as many as 20 nuclear families with small stock (sheep and goats) and cattle penned at night within the village fence. The majority of these farmers own or are part owners of herds of camels and flocks of sheep and goats tended by close kin in the best available pastures, often many miles from these farming settlements. Typically, a man with several wives will station one in a farming settlement with her children and flocks, while another is sent out with flocks of sheep and goats and some milch camels to distant pastures. Most of these farming settlements expand in population at harvest time or in the dry autumn months when sheep and goats return from the southern pastures in the Haud and Ogaden, and camels move closer to the dry season' homewells'. Village settlements are based on artificial ponds (singular, war) excavated and maintained collectively by the users who also regularly collaborate in harvesting. Each nuclear family has a plot of land of between a quarter and one acre in extent, of which usually only part is planted each year. Grass on the fallow land provides pasture for young stock and the stubble left after the harvest affords useful grazing for cattle in the dry winter months. Yields vary with the size of holding between 4 and 12 x 200 lb bags. Excess grain is stored in pit granaries dug in the centre of settlements.

22. Southern Cultivating Settlements

Unlike their northern counterparts, the Digil and Rahanweyn (and some Hawiye) who practise mixed farming along the banks and between the Juba and Shebelle Rivers in southern Somalia have a tradition of cultivation going back several centuries. The plough is not used traditionally in tilling the ground, this work being done instead by hand-hoe (*yambo*), in a system of cultivation which, according to some authorities is particularly well adapted to the inter-riverine soils, with their outstanding natural tilth. The chief crop in the dry-farming region of Bay is durra (sorghum:*misego* in Somali), whereas in the higher rainfall areas of middle and lower Shebelle the main crop is maize. (*gelay*). Subsidiary crops are: sesame (*simsim*), beans (*digir*) squashes (*bu'ur*) bananas (*muus*) cotton (*suuf*), sugar cane (*kassab*), groundnuts (*buuri*). Sesame is often planted after the spring *gu* rains and maize after the autumn *dayr* rains; sorghum is usually first planted after the *gu* and a second crop grown in the *dayr*. Both grains are stored in pit granaries where, although losing some of its value as seed, sorghum can keep for over ten years and still be suitable for domestic consumption. Most of the bananas which are so important for export and the sugar used for internal consumption are grown on estates, many of them privately owned, along the Shebelle and Juba Rivers. The oldest established riverine cultivators are people of mixed Somali and Swahili origin, some the descendants of former slaves imported from East Africa to serve as agricultural serfs for pastoral Somali landlords. Known as 'tough-haired' (*tima-adag*) and traditionally despised by the nomads, these people still provide the bulk of the unskilled labour force in the riverine plantation industry, and live in villages under headmen. They suffered terribly at the hands of Somali militia in the conflict of the early 1990s in southern Somalia.

In the dry farming upland Bay area, away from the rivers, villages *(bullo; bildan;* or *billed)* are based around ponds (singular, *war)*, owned by the man or men who organised the original work of excavation. There is a well established code of water management designed to safeguard the water and prevent its pollution by clothes washing, human defecation etc. Water-guards are organised at night, especially when water is scarce, and access granted only to members of the community. Similar co-operative parties provide the individual farmer with help in the heavy work of cultivation, clearing virgin bush, planting and harvesting and also in building the characteristic local mud and wattle hut *(mundille)*. Villages range in size from settlements of 20 to over a hundred houses, and nuclear or extended families. Village populations thus range from approximately 100-1000 men, women and children. The larger villages depend on several ponds and contain Quranic schools, mosques and other local facilities. Each married man, with about 3 dependents, normally has cultivating rights in at least one field. About 2 hectares of sorghum are planted in the spring rain season sometimes intercropped with cow peas. The corresponding yield in an average year is about 2,000 kg.

As in the case of small stock, women play an important role in cultivation—in planting, weeding and harvesting. The technique of cultivation is very distinctive. The field to be planted is first cleared of weeds and stubble from the previous season's crop. Once this has been done the field is divided into neat squares called *moos,* approximately 2m x 2m. Each side is two paces long. A strip of 40 or 50 squares constitutes the land measure known as a 'staff' *('ul).* A series of twelve such strips constitutes a plot known as a *darab* measuring approximately a quarter of a hectare. The squares have ridges to catch and retain rainwater so that the plot looks like a contoured or relief chessboard. The ridges are traditionally built with the aid of a heavy blunt wooden rake called *kewawa.* It is worked by a team of two men. One pushes with the handle while the other pulls from the opposite side with the attached rope. The man who is pushing the kewawa stands on the inside of the moos, shaping the loose top soil into a ridge while his companion stands outside, pulling the rope. The first man then turns at an angle of 45°, the other steps or jumps over to face him and they start on the next side. When that ridge is shaped the second man turns to face in his original direction, while the first moves to face him. This diagonal dance is carried on across the field, producing a step pattern of ridges. As this is crossed repeatedly it forms squares which eventually fill the field. This is heavy work.

It takes two men a full day's work to till a *darab* of land in this way. Sowing is another day's work. At least four days' work will be required for weeding, and one to three to harvest the crop. If, as is common when the rains are reasonable, both a spring and autumn crop are planted, the total minimum labour input required is thus of the order of 20 man days per *darab*. If two hectares (i.e. 8 *darabs*) are planted the minimum labour requirement is thus of the order of 160 man days. This, of course, makes no allowance for intercropping, ancillary weeding, driving off birds which attack the grain as it ripens, and the storage of the product in pit granaries, or its sale in market stores.

Despite the age of village settlements in this region and the heterogeneous character of the local Digil and Rahanweyn population, villages do not traditionally have headmen like those found amongst the Riverine population. Political allegiance, like land-rights, is ultimately vested in lineages, identification with which extends outside villages to the clan as both a territorial and kin group. Clan elders—at various times referred to as 'peace-seekers'—articulate with the government and authority of the day at District Headquarters level. Village solidarity, involving amongst other facilities the labour of the young men under a local leader, presents a potential for further local political organisation.

The majority of the Digil and Rahanweyn farmers also keep livestock, each family possessing, according to a 1977 FAO/World Bank report, on average 10 animal units (5 camels, 3 cattle, and 4 sheep and goats). Where, as is common, extended families have more livestock, the head of the family (the father or eldest of a group of brothers) stays at home on the farm, while younger kinsmen move semi-nomadically with cattle and animals.

True nomads (some of whom belong to the Digil and Rahan-weyn confederacies) also move through the inter-riverine region seasonally, often with large herds of camels. The most commonly seen are groups belonging to the Gaalje'el (the name means 'camel-lovers') and Garre* clans. The young camel-herders of these groups are known for their distinctive Afro-style hair-do called in Somali *guud*. Their herding settlements are organised in the same way as those described above for the northern nomads. As might be expected these people have much wider ranging movements and connections than the more sedentary Digil and Rahanweyn. The latter are additionally isolated by their distinctive speech *(Af-maymay)* which is not readily under-stood by other Somalis.

23. State Settlement Schemes following the 'Drought of the Long Tail'

Almost a quarter of a million nomads mainly from the north eastern region of the Republic lost most of their livestock in the devastating drought of 1974-1975. A large number of these des-titute pastoralists were established in state farms and fishing settlements, chiefly in the south. The largest agricultural settle-ments, with populations of approximately 20-30,000, were in the Lower Shebelle and Middle Juba** regions, with intensive cul-tivation based on irrigation and a considerable degree of mechanisation. These huge enterprises produced a mixture of crops including sorghum and rice, and had an elaborate and rather artificial social organisation purportedly designed to en-courage the process of detribalisation and the growth of patriotism. The organisation, in groups of family committees, was rather theoretical, while in actual practice there was more direction by officials of the relevant ministries which provided the necessary technical expertise. Families received rations,

* The Gaalje'el are usually classed as Hawiye, the Garre as Digil.
** The three main schemes were Kurtunwarre, Sablaale and Dujuma.

medical care, schooling and other social services and a small wage in return for their labour. Fishing settlements were established at Brava and elsewhere along the coast. These enterprises in which there was a more immediate return in the shape of regular fish catches were run as co-operatives, and the most successful appeared to be the smallest.

There are traditional precedents for transformation of Somali pastoral nomads into cultivators—not only in the case of those in Galbeed Region, but also in that of the Digil and Rahanweyn who in part derive from northern nomads who settled in the inter-river region over many centuries. There have also always been fishing communities on the Somali coasts, on the margins of the dominant nomadic culture. Although both represent occupations despised by the proud nomads, they have clearly often been adopted by pastoral drop-outs with no other hope of survival.

There was thus some precedent for the vast drought-relief settlement programme. The results, however, tended to illustrate the resilience of the pastoral culture. The agricultural settlements especially, lost a substantial proportion of the men who originally settled in them as destitute nomads. As the home grazing areas improved in the cycle of good seasons that so often follows a succession of drought years, men drifted back to resume herding, leaving women and children behind in the settlements where they received food, health care, and education. Some nomads saved enough from settlement wages, rations and other sources to send money to distant relatives, instructing them to invest in livestock on their behalf. In due course, when the makings of a new herd had been put together, men left the settlement covertly, and moved back to their familiar pastures where sheep and goats reproduce quickly under optimal conditions. Others joined the 'muscle-drain' of migrant workers in the Gulf States, an option which was eventually made less easy to pursue as the Somali government imposed tighter passport control. A similar, though less drastic exodus of men occurred from the fishing settlements where there was at least a protein catch to substitute for livestock, and where conditions, especially in the smaller co-operatives, were less regimented.

24. The Refugee Crisis (1978-80)

The vast exodus of ethnic Somali and related Oromo (Galla) and other peoples from Western Somalia/Eastern Ethiopia in the wake of the 1977/78 Ogaden war, imposed an even more crippling burden on the SDR than the natural disaster of 1974. As the guerrilla war waged by the Western Somali Liberation Front and their allies the Abo and Oromo Liberation Fronts continued, the influx of refugees became overwhelming. From some 400,000 refugees registered in camps in December 1979, a year later the figure had more than doubled, with a corresponding increase in the number of camps to over 30. Outside the camps as many as another half million were estimated to have found hospitality as 'invisible refugees' living with relatives, further straining the fragile economy of the SDR with its acute foreign exchange problems. By the end of 1980 virtually one out of every four people in the SDR was a refugee; the fact that the majority of refugees were ethnic Somalis with kinsmen in the Republic blurred the otherwise appalling impact of this statistic. The paradox was that these pathetically uprooted war victims were refugees in a State based on their own ethnic identity: they were, as it were, refugees 'at home'. But their real home, to which they sought to return, was the Ogaden, and, in the case of Oromo refugees, Sidamo and Bale provinces of Ethiopia.

Transit reception camps were set up at key points on the border with Ethiopia, and the main camps—containing up to 50,000 people—were further inside Somalia's borders. The character of the camps' population partly reflected what might be called the political demography of the refugee situation. The large number of UN and other agency surveys in the camps found that the majority of refugees were women, young children and old men. Most of the men-folk who had camels still surviving in the Ogaden stayed there with their herds. This applied particularly to the young men—the traditional camel-boys and warriors—who remained behind with these livestock and lent their support to the Western Somali Liberation Front guerrillas. Thus the demographic make-up of the camp populations reflected the traditional division of labour and herding units in the nomadic economy. Other refugees outside the camps did in some cases bring their livestock, especially small stock (sheep and goats) with them. The presence of this additional animal population, while providing food, also increased the erosion of scarce grazing in the Republic, and the wood and charcoal cooking-fuel needs of all the refugees led to further serious pressure on the country's limited forest and scrub bush resources. Indeed, by the end of 1980, it was proving necessary to import fuel for domestic cooking in the camps.

While external humanitarian and governmental agencies played a crucial role in trying to feed and clothe the refugees as well as providing medical supplies, the SDR early responded to this crisis in an exemplary fashion. Relief work was organised by the Somali Refugee Commission, directed by the Minister of Local Government and Rural Development. Over 2,000 Somali personnel from most of the country's ministries were involved in this task on which by July 1980 the Somali government had expended over £16 million from its own slender resources. The humanitarian needs of the refugees received initially little publicity—despite Somali efforts—and it took many months for the international community to register the magnitude of the calamity and respond appropriately.

As far as the internal organisation of the main refugee camps was concerned, they were divided into sections or quarters—which were usually named by the refugees after places in the Ogaden from which the refugees derived. At the same time, efforts were made by the government to introduce the same scheme of decimal divisions and sub-divisions of communities (over-riding traditional clan divisions) which had been imposed in the agricultural and fishing settlements established for the victims of the 1974 drought.

Although some efforts, with varying degrees of success, were made to promote cultivation, poultry-keeping and crafts in some of the camps, none was anywhere near being self-sufficient. The stark fact remained that the economy of the SDR simply did not possess the resources to absorb so many uprooted people, even when the majority were ethnically Somali and indeed kinsmen.

This major economic aspect of the refugee situation was reinforced by the political aspiration—on the part of the refugees themselves as much as the government of the SDR—to return to the country from which they had been forced to flee by what they saw as Ethiopian imperialism. After all, the Ogaden region takes its name from the Somali people who traditionally inhabit it and whose drive for self-determination did not necessarily mean an unqualified desire to merge with the Republic.

Part Four: War and Famine

25. Internal Dissent after the Ogaden War

At its height the Ogaden war (see ch.15) had been immensely popular in Somalia and President Siyad's public standing never higher. The terrible defeat and refugee invasion (which seriously upset the existing clan demography) quickly led to widespread public demoralisation and to an upsurge of 'tribalism' (i.e. clan loyalties) as different groups sought scapegoats to explain the debacle. Thus, hard on the heels of the Somali retreat, an unsuccessful attempted coup was mounted against the regime in April 1978. This was led by military officers of the Mijerteyn (Darod) clan who had played a dominant role in the old civilian governments. After the failure of this attempted coup, those who had escaped arrest regrouped, forming a guerrilla opposition group called the Somali Salvation Democratic Front (SSDF) which made its operational headquarters across the border in Ethiopia. After some initial successes—with Ethiopian support—this organisation and its clan-base in Somalia was savagely subdued. That the Mijerteyn sought support in Ethiopia, Somalia's traditional enemy, is both a sign of their desperation and a measure of the degree of disintegration of Somali national solidarity. All the measures of Siyad's Scientific Socialism had evidently not after all succeeded in their task of transforming Somali national solidarity from the ancient 'mechanical' to the modern 'organic' mode (to borrow Durkheim's terminology).

In 1989-90, the spotlight fell on the main protagonist in the recent civil war in Somalia, the Somali National Movement (SNM) which, despite its name, drew most of its support from the Isaq clans of central northern Somalia and articulated their profound disaffection in regard to the Siyad regime. Following the example of the SSDF, the SNM was able to make its operational headquarters across the border in Ethiopia from which it launched a number of daring raids. From the early 1980s, the north was administered by increasingly harsh military rule emanating from the capital, with savage reprisals meted out to the assumedly pro-SNM local population who were subject to severe economic as well as political harassment. The north, as I saw when I last visited it in 1985, began to look and feel like a downtrodden colony under a foreign military tyranny.

Armed opposition to Siyad was spreading and assuming a national character transcending clan divisions. But, at the same time, despite their common objective—the overthrow of Siyad—the predominantly Darod and Isaq bases, respectively, of the SSDF and SNM added to their other logistical and leadership difficulties preventing them from making common cause and so weakened the overall impact of their rebellion.

Since the Ogaden War defeat, Siyad had still continued to support, albeit somewhat nominally, the Ogadeeni Western Somali Liberation Front which remained an irksome thorn in Ethiopia's side. However, the destabilising pressures exerted by the SSDF and SNM had the effect of driving President Siyad to seek an accommodation with Ethiopia, a move which was also encouraged by Somalia's Western allies (Italy, the EEC, and the USA). The Somali regime's anxiety to secure a deal with Ethiopia was increased by the insecurity that his clansmen felt when the President had a nearly fatal car crash in May 1986. Siyad, nevertheless, proved remarkably resilient, and at the end of that year was re-elected, unopposed, (since no opposition was permitted) as head of state for a further seven year term. A new government was formed in February 1987. For the first time since the coup, however, the cabinet now included a 'Prime Minister' in the curious shape of the faithful General Samatar (Siyad's long-serving and politically unassuming military commander). In reality, however, President Siyad had consolidated the position of his own clan and family within which rivalry over who should eventually succeed him was beginning to become acute. The Marrehan now unquestionably and openly dominated the military, and Siyad's unprepossessing son, General Masleh, was put in charge of a special northern command unit. The old MOD alliance was beginning to crumble, at least at the highest levels, as the Marrehan closed ranks in the face of mounting insecurity. The time had come to secure Ethiopian co-operation in cauterising the SNM and SSDF.

26. Peace with Ethiopia, Chaos at Home

Further signalling the demise of pan-Somali solidarity, in April 1988, President Siyad and Ethiopia's Mengistu Haile Marian finally signed a peace accord, normalising their relations and undertaking to stop supporting each other's dissidents. Thus Siyad withdrew support from the WSLF (which was by now opposed by an anti-Siyad organisation—the Ogaden National Liberation Front), and Mengistu formally withdrew support from the SSDF and SNM. Knowledge of this detente and fear of its consequences triggered the latter's audacious onslaught on military installations in Northern Somalia, which quickly led to the 1988-91 all-out civil war between the regime and the Isaq clansmen.

The human cost was terrible. Thousands of civilians were killed and wounded, and at least half a million fled their homes seeking asylum across the border in Ethiopia and in the Republic of Djibouti. Thousands of refugees eventually found refuge in Canada, Britain, Scandinavia, Italy and the USA. Meanwhile, male Ogadeni refugees in northern Somalia, who had long been subject to illegal recruitment into Siyad's armed forces, were conscripted as a paramilitary militia to fight the SNM and to man checkpoints on the roads. Ogadeni refugees were encouraged to take over the remains of Isaqi shops and houses in what, after their bombardment by Siyad's forces, were effectively ghost towns. Thus, those who had been earlier received as refugee guests in northern Somalia had supplanted their Isaqi hosts; and many of the latter, in this bitterly ironic turn of fate, had become refugees in the Ogaden.

If the Ogadenis were once the tail that wagged the dog, drawing Somalia into their fight for liberation from Ethiopian rule, the situation in 1989-90 was very different. Those still in the Ogaden were to all intents and purposes deserted by Siyad while those outside in Somalia were co-opted into fighting to maintain the regime. Here the appeal, also addressed to the disunited Mijerteyn, was for Darod solidarity against the Isaq. Thus other northern Darod clans were armed by the regime and urged to join the fight. Other northern groups (such as the Esa and

Gadabursi) who are neither Isaq nor Darod, were also armed and exhorted to turn against the Isaq. The regime's appeal for Darod solidarity evoked a corresponding attempt by the Isaq to invoke a wider-based, higher level 'Irrir' solidarity to include the important Hawiye clans in whose territory Mogadishu, the capital of the Republic, is located. While seeking Darod support where appropriate, the regime also endeavoured to secure the loyalty of all non-Isaq clans and, of course, to penetrate the ranks of the Isaq. Thus, in its desperate fight for survival, Siyad's family and clansmen sought to exploit to the full segmentary lineage rivalry within the Somali nation. They also made abundant use of coercion and rewards of all kinds, as corruption flourished.

By the end of January 1991, the SNM had effectively overcome Siyad's forces in the north and was consolidating its position throughout the region. Many Ogadeni refugees had returned to their kinsmen in Ethiopia, who were now incorporated in three new 'autonomous' regions within the Ethiopian state. Other mutinous Ogadeni soldiery in southern Somalia had established the Somali Patriotic Movement in 1989 which joined the loose coalition of movements fighting Siyad, particularly the recently formed United Somali Congress.

Partly derived from an earlier association with the SNM, the USC had become primarily a Hawiye organisation with two main factions, one based on the Abgal clan, whose home town was the Somali capital, Mogadishu, and the other based on the Habar Gidir, the clan of the USC militia commander, General Aideed (himself a former general in Siyad's army and ex-ambassador to India). Siyad, of course, sought to exploit these divisions as well as exhorting all the Darod in Mogadishu to kill the Hawiye citizens whether they were Abgal or Habar Gidir. The ensuing inter-clan violence, however, threatened Siyad's position further, and in desperation he finally turned his heavy artillery on the Hawiye quarters of the city. This provoked the extremely bloody general uprising which led to Siyad's flight from the town on 26th January 1991, pursued by General Aideed who had recently entered Mogadishu with his forces.

While Aideed was thus engaged chasing Siyad, the USC Abgal group in Mogadishu hastily set up an 'interim government' under Ali Mahdi (a prominent Abgal businessman) as provisional president and with Ministers drawn from the members of other (non-Hawiye) clans—not all of whom had actually been consulted, far less accepted office! When this, largely self-appointed, administration began to try to control the numerous armed groups at large in Mogadishu, the Habar Gidir became suspicious of Abgal intentions and fighting erupted between the two Hawiye clans. With the calling of a USC party congress in July 1991, at which Aideed was elected USC Chairman, with Ali Mahdi continuing as 'Interim President', an uneasy peace was restored.

Meanwhile, Siyad and his remaining henchmen had fled to his clan territory in Gedo where he proceeded to attempt to mobilise and manipulate pan-Darod solidarity, forming the Marrehan-based 'Somali National Front'. Appeals to Darod unity were encouraged by the indiscriminate revenge killings of people of this clan-family (especially those of the Dulbahante clan associated with the NSS) perpetrated by Hawiye groups in the aftermath of Siyad's escape from Mogadishu. Thus a motley group of Darod-based forces (including, for a time, some SPM and SSDF as well as Marrehan) became engaged in a series of skirmishes with USC forces in the area between Mogadishu and the port of Kismayu to the south, and Afgoi and Baidoa to the west and north. In April 1991, after heavy fighting and at the cost of a renewed exodus to Ethiopia and Kenya of thousands of Darod refugees, the USC gained control of Kismayu—losing it again later in the year, but recovering it in the spring of 1992. Not all the Darod, of course, were engaged in this conflict and far from decisively defeated: the position of the important Mijerteyn clan and its SSDF remained at this time still equivocal—partly because some of the Mijerteyn lived in the Kismayu hinterland, far from their headquarters in the north-east. By the summer of 1991, and along similar lines to developments in the north-west, the whole region occupied by the Mijerteyn in the north-east (Bari, Nugal and Mudug provinces) had become effectively self-governing under SSDF administration.

Returning to the situation in Mogadishu, by September the

MAIN SOMALI CLANS AND MOVEMENTS 1992/1993

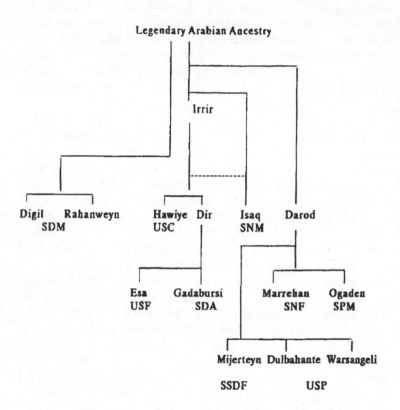

Note: USC main divisions are: Aideed faction/Habar Gidir clan; Ali Mahdi faction/Abgal clan. USC Aideed faction, and SPM led by Omer Jess are part of the alliance called SNA (Somali National Alliance).

Somali Movements 1992/1993

DAROD	Marrehan	Somali National Front
	Ogaden	Somali Patriotic Movement (two main branches: Muhamed Zubayr lineages led by General Aden Abdallahi Nur (Gabio); other lineages groupsled by Colonel Ahmed Umar Jess)
	Mijerteyn	Somali Salvation Democratic Front
	Dulbahante	United Somali Party
	Warsangeli	United Somali Party
DIGIL & RAHANWEYN		Somali Democratic Movement
DIR	'Ise	United Somali Front
	Gadabursi	Somali Democratic Alliance
	Southern Dir Clans	Southern Somali National Movement
HAWIYE	Abgal	United Somali Congress led by Ali Mahdi
	Habar Gidir	United Somali Congress led by General Aideed
ISAQ	All Isaq Clans	Somali National Movement

USC conflict had flared up again. Mogadishu was now effectively divided into two principal military zones—one controlled by the Abgal and the other by the Habar Gidir.

Other smaller Hawiye groups maintained their own zones of influence, with their militia, sometimes acting as neutrals, sometimes as partisan allies in the ensuing blood-bath which between November 1991 and April 1992 had almost completely devastated what remained of Mogadishu after Siyad's ravages, causing death and injury to civilians on a catastrophic scale and plunging the whole area into chaos and famine. The most effective ceasefire between the two sides, in April 1992, coincided significantly with Siyad's abortive attempt to recapture Mogadishu for the Marrehan.

27. The Rebirth of Somaliland

During this long period of confused clan manoeuvring and turmoil in the south, the USC 'interim government' in Mogadishu sent its Isaq prime minister and other ministers on largely fruitless missions abroad to seek international aid and recognition.

Appreciating that external recognition would require widespread internal support, Ali Mahdi's government tried at the same time to persuade the SNM and other movements to join in talks aimed at the formation of an acceptable national government. Most publicly, this was pursued at the abortive Djibouti conferences of July 1991. That the USC 'Prime Minister', Omer Arteh, was a well-known Isaq figure might have been expected to facilitate these complex negotiations. Actually this had the reverse effect. He had been appointed without consultation with the SNM who, in any case, regarded him as tainted by a too close association with Siyad, as well as possessing other negative features. Hence the SNM, whose links with the USC were in any case through Aideed and the Habar Gidir rather than Ali Mahdi, responded coolly to these overtures. This cautious response seemed amply justified as the extent of internal USC divisions became plain in the developing conflict and chaos in and around Mogadishu.

So, the SNM concentrated on its own local problems in the north. A surprising degree of peace between the Isaq and non-Isaq clans of the region (the former British Somaliland Protectorate) had been secured, largely through the efforts of the traditional clan elders, by the time of the SNM national congress in May 1991. There was widespread hatred and distrust of the south (identified with Siyad's misrule) and a strong tide of public feeling favouring separatism. Bowing to this, the SNM leadership proclaimed on 18th May 1991 that their region would resume its independence from the south, taking the title 'Somaliland Republic'. This pragmatic decision reflected the desire of many of the people of Somaliland to get on with rebuilding their country and ruined towns, after their devastation by Siyad's forces which had left hundreds of thousands of landmines to remind northerners of that barbaric regime.

The Somali Republic had thus now reverted to its two former constituent colonial units—the ex-British and ex-Italian Somalilands—a development that was bitterly, but ineffectually, opposed by Ali Mahdi's administration in Mogadishu. There were now two interim governments—neither of which recognised the other—and each of which desperately sought international emergency aid and diplomatic recognition. While the SNM government had, initially, virtually countrywide support, Ali Mahdi's government was effectively restricted to the Mogadishu area and after September 1991 to only a dwindling part of the town itself. Outside Mogadishu, various locally-based clan forces reigned and struggled for control of wider areas.

The same tendencies of reversion to clan relative loyalties, with the alliance and disassociation of segmentary kin-groups according to the political context. characterised the general scene throughout the Somali region in 1992. Siyad's much publicised official campaigns against clan allegiance had absolutely no positive lasting effect, which was perhaps not surprising since they were essentially rhetorical. Indeed, Siyad's own power politics always included a powerful clan element and served to reinforce and exacerbate ancient antagonisms in the segmentary lineage system—which, of course, he did not invent. He well knew, however, how to adapt the ancient divide-and-rule formula to these particular clan conditions. He befriended groups which enabled him to attack his clan enemies. In this pattern of what has been aptly called (clan) clientelism', Siyad distributed arms and money to his friends, encouraging them to attack their common clan enemies who, of course, were accused of divisive 'tribalism' by the master tribalist. The legacy of his rule, including the making of peace with Ethiopia (thus removing this factor of external threat), contributed materially to the ensuing post-Siyad-period situation in which the Somali nation became more deeply divided along its traditional kinship lines than perhaps at any other time this century. Here we might say that if the segmentary system had not already existed, Siyad would have invented it to cling to power at the vortex of clan chaos. By destroying his country's economy, Siyad also directly promoted those conditions of general lack of resources and insecurity on which clan loyalty thrives, since clan solidarity offers the only hope of survival. Also by providing arms—directly and indirectly, Siyad's legacy of Marrehan misrule ensured a wide and persistent prevalence of extremely bloody clan conflict.

The pan-Somali ideal, founded in cultural identity rather than political unity evoked in opposition to the colonial situation, which was so strong in the 1950s and 1960s has taken a severe battering. In 1991/92, reactively influenced by the example of the SSDF, the SNM, USC and SPM, the general tendency was for every major Somali clan to form its own militia movement. Thus clans are becoming effectively self-governing entities throughout the Somali region as they carve out spheres of influence in a process which, with the abundance of modern weapons, frequently entails bitter conflicts with a high toll of civilian casualties.

The political geography of the Somali hinterland in 1992, consequently, closely resembled that reported by European explorers in the 19th century, with spears replaced by Kalashnikovs and bazukas. The clan areas could only be entered or traversed by outsiders, i.e. people of other clans and foreigners, with the consent of the locals and, usually, the payment of appropriate fees for 'protection'. This is the situation confronting those intrepid non-governmental agencies which still operate in the area.

As further illustration, the story is told by a well-respected former Somali Minister of the Interior who, on 7th January 1992 set off from Mogadishu, leading a road convoy of over seventy vehicles bound for the north, and arrived at Burao exactly a month later—a journey which used to take some twenty-four hours to accomplish along the Chinese-built tarmac road. The convoy had its own paid armed escorts, and in addition was forced to hire local guides and protectors while traversing different clan areas; four vehicles were looted *en route*—one by the convoy's armed escort when it had completed its mission; other vehicles had to be abandoned, and only fifty-one reached their final destination—with the help of donations of fuel from the Red Cross and Save the Children Fund. Accidents in the course of this remarkable journey accounted for eighteen deaths and about thirty injured people. On the other hand, nine babies were born in the course of the journey

Clan politics, however, has never been characterised by hard and fast alliances that are limited to the clan level. Related clans can and do, according to circumstances, ally in wider formations. So, as we have seen, the USC faction leaders in Mogadishu, however divided amongst themselves internally are preceived externally as Hawiye, which tends to trigger a reactive alliance of other groups, for example a coalescing of the various Darod clan movements at a higher level of Darod unity, and similarly among the Isaq clans of the north. By the same token, the tensions and conflicts which have broken out among the latter in the Somaliland Republic's first years of existence are linked to the fact that once the Isaq had made peace with their non-Isaq neighbours (the Gadabursi, Dulbahante and Warsangeli) they were more likely to be divided internally. Their largely successful resolution of conflict to date, however—mainly by panels of local clan elders—is remarkable.

28. International Intervention

Outside Somaliland and further south, order only existed in the SSDF-controlled north-east region, largely thanks to the close relationship between this Front and the local Mijerteyn clan elders. Thus by 1992, southern Somalia had become a war zone, undermined by years of nepotistic abuse and deprived of foreign aid, the economy had completely collapsed, most foreign missions and the UN had left the country, and only a few daring NGOs (such as Medecin Sans Frontiers, the Red Cross, and Save the Children) remained to provide succour for some of the victims of the spiralling civil war. Equipped with vast quantities of arms, the forces of the two rival USC 'war-lords', General Aideed and Ali Mahdi, tore Mogadishu apart as well as fighting Siyad's regrouped clan militia, the Somali National Front, for control of the southern coast and hinterland. Their various engagements imported war and devastation to the grain-farming region between the rivers, spreading famine throughout southern Somalia. Attempts to land relief food at Mogadishu port and distribute it to the hinterland were undermined by extensive looting and the rake-offs systematically levied by the militias which sought food not only for their members but also to sell in order to buy *qat* and arms. Thus the humanitarian agencies themselves were inadvertently sucked into the conflict and became factors in the general 'problem'.

When the UN returned in April 1992 with a dynamic special representative, Mohamed Sahnoun, appointed by the Secretary General, it was not equipped to undertake the required level of armed intervention needed to secure effective aid distribution. It was left to the US in December 1992 to impose peace on the warring factions and foster a new active interventionist role for the UN. 'Operation Restore Hope' did secure food supplies and short-term conflict containment, and paved the way for the unique UN peace-enforcement military administration, UNOSOM 2, which followed on in Spring 1993 when the 'war-lords' agreed in Addis Ababa on peace and disarmament and on the formation of interim political structures. The new special representative Admiral Howe, an American and former US security adviser, heading UNOSOM 2 was to oversee the implementation of the agreements with a multinational force, commanded by a Turkish general, and which, although it could draw on US back-up forces, was considerably smaller than Operation Restore Hope. By June, without any substantial progress towards disarmament and new supplies of weapons, Aideed's forces challenged the new arrangements. A fierce attack was launched on a party of Pakistani soldiers of the UN force, and over twenty were killed. This provoked the UN Security Council into a sharp denunciation of Aideed and the other warlords as guilty of war crimes. Aideed's headquarters and arms stores in Mogadishu were attacked by US helocopters and, in the ensuing reaction by his supporters, fierce clashes occurred in which there were considerable civilian casualties.

SUGGESTED READING

[Publisher's Note: Many of the references which appeared in the earlier edition of this book have been retained in the following list even though some will only be obtainable from libraries. The decision to continue their inclusion was so as to provide historical documentation of their sometime existence for the benefit of present and future researchers and others who may be interested.]

Traditional Culture

A.A. Abokor, *The Camel in Somali Oral Traditions*, Uppsala, 1987

B.W. Andrzejewski and I. M. Lewis, *Somali Poetry*, Oxford, 1964, (out of print) offers a brief introduction to traditional Somali culture and translates Somali poems which reflect this background.

B.W. Andrzejewski with S. Andrzejewski, *An Anthology of Somali Poetry*, Bloomington, 1993. A new collection of Somali poetry, translated by B.W. Andrzejewski and his wife.

Richard Burton's *First Footsteps in East Africa*, recording the author's expedition from Zeila to Harar in 1854, first published in 1856, remains a vivid and accurate account of many features of traditional Somali culture

Muusa Galaal's *Terminology and Practice of Somali Weatherlore, Astronomy and Astrolology*, Mogadishu (cyclostyled) 1968, provides a fascinating insight into the traditional weather-lore of Somali nomads. Muusa Galaal was, of course, the most distinguished poet and expert on Somali language and culture.

J.W. Johnson's *Heelooy, heeleellooy: the development of Genre Heello in modern Somali Poetry*, Indiana 1974, shows how contemporary popular poetry cast in the idiom of love songs offers a lively political commentary on events.

S.S. Samatar, *Oral Poetry and Somali Nationalism*, Cambridge, 1982. A brilliant study by the Professor of African History at Rutgers University of the crucial role of poetry in Somali politics, especially in the case of the Somali jihad-leader, Seyyid Mohammad Abdille Hassan.

General Ethnograhic Features

A.M. Abdullahi, *Pastoral Production Systems in Africa:* a study of nomadic household economy and livestock marketing in Central Somalia, Kiel, 1990

D. R. Aronson, 'Kinsmen and comrades: towards a class analysis of the Somali Pastoral Sector', *Nomadic Peoples, No. 7,* November, 1980, pp. 14-24, develops this argument further. Aronson examines the profits being made by middlemen and large-scale stock exporters.

J.A. Hunt's *A General Survey of the Somaliland Protectorate,* 1944-50, London (Crown Agents) 1957, provides excellent detailed information on the physical environment, its resources, and nomadic movements in the north.

I. M. Lewis's *A Pastoral Democracy,* London 1961 (reprint 1981) is a detailed social anthropological analysis of northern Somali nomadism in the late 1950s. It includes material on the cultivators in the north-west. The same author's paperback, *Social Anthropology in Perspective* , Cambridge University Press, 1985,makes frequent reference to the Somalis.

I.M. Lewis *Peoples of the Horn of Africa,* London (International African Institute) 1955 and 1969; to be re-published by HAAN Associates 1993: Provides a detailed picture of Somali life, social institutions and general culture. It also contains an exhaustive (up to 1960) bibliography. The book is based on a survey of sources published prior to 1954: it does not include any of the results of its author's own fieldwork begun in 1955. Extensive use is made of the pioneering studies of the great Italian scholar, Enrico Cerulli, whose collected works on Somalia were printed in three volumes, and published in Rome 1957 and 1959 with the title *Somalia: scritti vari editi ed inediti*

I.M. Lewis, *Blood and Bone: the call of kinship in Somali society,* New Jersey, 1993. This book brings together a series of related studies of different aspects of Somali kinship ideology and behaviour in northern and southern Somalia. It explores how Somalis use kinship as a 'natural' vehicle for all forms of joint interest, economic as well as political. The last two chapters examine current Somali politics at the 'national' level. Pastoral Nomadism

J. Swift, 'Pastoral development in Somalia' in M. H. Glantz (ed.), *Desertification: environmental degradation in and around arid lands,* Boulder 1977, contains some interesting speculations on socio-economic change among the northern nomads

Southern Cultivating Somali

R.. Antoniotto 'The Fishing Settlement at Baraawe: Notes on Cultural Adaptation', in *Somalia and the World, Vol. 2,* 1979, pp. 237-250 and E. Forni, 'Woman's New Role and Status in the Baraawe Settlement' in *Somalia and the World,* pp. 251-265 provide useful documentation on the fishing settlement at Brava.

The best general sociological analysis here is still M. Colucci's *Principi di diritto Consuetudinario della Somalia italiana meridionale,* Florence 1924.

J. M. Haakonsen, *Scientific Socialism and Self-Reliance,* Rome, 1980 provides interesting information on the fishing co-operatives, based on a short preliminary study.

The most important modern anthropological study of a southern Somali group is B. Helander's *The Slaughtered Camel: coping with fictitious descent among the Huber of southern Somalia,* Stockholm 1993.

For a detailed study of the Geledi of Afgoi and their famous annual 'stick-fight' see V. Luling, 'The Social Structure of Southern Somali Tribes', unpublished PhD thesis, University of London, 1971.

Settlement Schemes for nomads

G. Massey, *Subsistence and change: Lessons of Agropastoralism in Somalia,* Boulder, 1987. A valuable survey study of village production in southern Somalia.

There are numerous reports by different organisations at different stages, on the refugee camps and the food, health and other needs of the refugees. On the medical side two of the most useful are probably: S. P. Simmonds, *'Appropriate Health Services with Refugees—with particular reference to*

Somalia', UK African Studies Association Symposium on Refugees, September 1979; *Report of the Center for Disease Control: Epidemiology team to the Refugee Health Unit, Ministry of Health*, SDR, June, 1980.]

History

L. V. Cassanelli, *The Shaping of Somali Society: reconstructing the history of a pastoral people*, 1600-1900, University of Pennsylvania Press, 1982. Based on oral and written sources, this is a pioneering study of southern Somalia over three centuries.

Margaret Castagno, *Historical Dictionary of Somalia*, New Jersey, 1975, offers a useful guide.

N. Chittick, 'An archaeological reconnaissance in the Horn: The British-Somali Expedition, 1975', *Azania, Vol. XI*, 1976, pp. 117-133, provides a rare and indispensable survey of the current archaeological situation in Somalia.

L. W. Doob's *Resolving Conflict in Africa*, New Haven 1970, describes how a workshop for intellectuals from Somalia, Ethiopia and Kenya attempted to find a solution to the Somali dispute.

J. Drysdale, *The Somali Dispute*, London and New York, 1964; a standard work on the Pan-Somali issue.

Ali Abdirahman Hersi's *The Arab Factor in Somali History* (PhD thesis, University of California, Los Angeles, 1977) provides a unique assessment of the Arabian connexion in Somalia, making extensive use of previously neglected Arabic sources.

R. L. Hess's *Italian Colonialism in Somalia*, Chicago 1966, provides a useful history of Italian rule in pre-independence Somalia.

D. Laitin & S. S. Samatar, *Somalia: Nation in search of a state*, Boulder, 1987. A valuable general account of Somali history, especially since independence in 1960.

M. de Lancy, S.L. Elliot, December Green et al, 'Somalia' in *World Bibliographic Series, Vol. 92*, 1988: Useful guide.

I. M. Lewis's *A Modern History of Somalia: nation and state in the Horn of Africa*, Boulder, 1988, is a comprehensive political history of Somali affairs from pre- to post-independence.

Mohamed Osman Omar, *The Road to Zero: Somalia's self-destruction*, London 1992. A 'life and times' social history account by a former chief of protocol and diplomat, of the period 1950's to the overthrow of Siyad Barre.

A.I. Samatar, *Socialist Somalia: Rhetoric and Reality* London 1988. An assessment of the 'socialist' era in Somalia.

A.I. Samatar, *The State and Rural Transformation in Northern Somalia*, 1884-1986, Madison, 1989. A marxist account of economic change amongst the 'peasant' cultivators of northwest Somalia.

Africa Watch, *Somalia: A Government at War with its own People*, London 1990. Partisan account of Siyad's campaigns against the population of northern Somalia.

A. Sheikh-Abdi, *Divine Madness: Mohammed Abdulle Hassan (1856-1920)*, London 1993. A new evaluation of the Seyyid, including some previously untranslated poetry.

For those who can read Somali, the highly original works of the self-taught Somali historian, Sheikh Aw Jama Umar Ise, are especially important for the Dervish period (1900-1920). See also Y.I. Kenadiid, *Ina Abdille Hassan*, 1984.

For Current Information

See: the international journal *Horn of Africa*; *Horn of Africa Bulletin*, Life and Peace Institute, Uppsala; the *Anglo-Somali Society Journal*; and reports by Africa Watch and Amnesty International, and by various UK NGOs.

The American State Department publication, *Area Handbook* is also a useful source of information.

On the self-declared Somaliland Republic (the former British Protectorate) see J. Drysdale *Somaliland 1991*: Report and Reference, Hove 1992.

Novels

Nuruddin Farah, *From a Crooked Rib*, London, 1970. *A Naked Needle* (a view of contemporary Mogadishu) London 1976. *Sweet and Sour Milk* (set in mid-1970s Somalia) London, 1980. These are just some of the titles by Nuruddin Farah, a

Somali novelist who writes in English. His most recent novel, *Gifts,* is published in the UK by Serif, 1993.

Marion Molteno, *A Shield of Coolest Air,* London 1992, about Somali refugee families in the UK.

Language and Linguistics

The major international authority is B. W. Andrzejewski, Professor Emeritus, School of Oriental and African Studies, London. His publications are listed in: B. W. Andrzejewski, 'The role of indicator particles in Somali', *Afroasiatic Linguistics, Vol. I, part 6,* pp. 1-69, 1975; 'The development of a national orthography in Somalia and the modernisation of the Somali language', *Horn of Africa, 1978, vol. I, part 3.*

A.A. Issa, *Somali Common Expressions,* Maryland 1987.

A.A. Issa & R.D. Zore, *Somali Textbook,* Maryland 1991

David D. Laitin's *Politics, Language and Thought,* Chicago 1977, explores the relationship between Somali ethnic identity and the use of the national language as oral and written medium.

Husseyn M. Adam's Master's thesis (University of Makerere 1969) *A Nation in Search of a Script,* recounts the problems involved in choosing a script for Somali.

Omar Osman Mohamed's *From Written Somali to a Rural Development Campaign* (SIDAM, Mogadishu 1975) recounts the successful literacy campaigns using the Latin (i e. English) script, adopted by the Siyad government in 1972.

Glossary of Terms

Conventional Anglicised spelling of the Somali word is used in some instance to assist the reader who is unfamiliar with the Somali orthography to achieve a close approximation of the pronunciation.

'aano (caano)	milk
adi	sheep and goats (collective term)
Af-maymay	dialect spoken by Digil and Rahanweyn
aqal	collapsable nomad's tent
ardaa wadaag	camel herdsmen's communal sleeping mat
aros (aroos)	marriage house
bah	uterine family
bahweyn/minweyn	senior wife
baraka	religious power possessed by religious leaders and teachers, and believed by Somalis to be inherited as well as achieved
bariis	rice
barkad	cement-lined water tank
bildan/billed/bullo	villages
buri	tobacco
burnuq	sweet potatoes
bu'ur	squashes
dangalo	co-wife/jealousy
darab	measure of cultivated land
dayr	autumn
degmo	grazing encampment (from deg: to settle)
diir/digir	beans
diya	blood compensation (also mag)
dumaal	widow inheritance

gel (geel)	camels
gelay	maize
guri	nomad domestic group (from gur: to move)
gu'	spring (season)
guud	hairstyle of Gaaljecel and Garre clansmen
haas/raas (xaas)	uterine family
haasas/raasas (xaasas)	polygynous family
heer (xeer)	treaty, contract
heerka qoyska (xeerka)	family law
hiddid (xiddid)	ties established by marriage
higsisan (xigsiisan)	replacement wife (for widower)
jaalle	friend, comrade. (N.B. This word became so inextricably associated with the most hated aspects of the Barre regime that it has lost acceptable usage.)
qassab	sugarcane
kewawa	heavy blunt wooden rake used in cultivation
laws (loows)	groundnuts
mahar (meher)	witnessed marriage contract
mal (maal)	capital (particularly livestock)
misego	sorghum
mod	disposable wealth
moos	squares of cultivated land (2m x 2m)
muus	bananas
mundille	mud and wattle hut
Nabad-doon	peace-seekers
oday(al)	elder(s) (also 'duk' and 'akhyaar')
qat	*catha edulis*: the leaves of this plant, imported in bundles from Kenya and Ethiopia, which look like English privet hedge, and chewed for their stimulant properties.

qabila	clan (Arabic)
reer	group, people
reer guura	grazing camel units (i.e. nomads)
saar	spirit possession illness (mainly in women)
simsim	sesame
sonkorqan	sweet potatoes
sultan(s) (suldhaan(o)	dynastic head (also 'ugas', 'gerad', 'boqor')
suf (suuf)	cotton
tima adag	agricultural serfs, literally coarse-haired'
tol	clan descent (hence 'tolayn', nationalisation)
ul	40 or 50 'moos' (measure of land)
'urad (curad)	first-born children
wadad(s) waddaad(o)	sheikh(s) religious leader(s), teacher(s)
war	artificial pond used by nomads or cultivators
yambo	hand-hoe
yarad	marriage payments from groom's to wife's group

CHRONOLOGY

This outline is based on written documentary material and excludes the earlier 'pre-history' of the region.

9/10th centuries AD	Arab families settled in ports along Somali coast spreading Islam
12th century AD	Northern Somali clans spread southwards (having probably fanned out into the Horn from an earlier movement northwards in the first millenaeum AD)
14th century	Arab traveller,Ibn Battuta, provides vivid contemporary descriptions of life in the towns of Zeila and Mogadishu.
1540/1560	First detailed reference in written chronicles to Somali people and component clans and time of great Muslim champion, Ahmed Gurey (Gran), leader of *jihad* against Christian Ethiopian kingdom. Somali warriors in his forces described as being especially expert at road ambushes.
17th century	Inhabitants of coastal town of Mogadishu, with predominant Arab and Persian influence, under pressure from Hawiye Somali (Abgal) of the hinterland, who settled in Shangani quarter of the city. This was followed by a period of Omani influence along the southern Somali coast.
1846-48	French explorer Charles Guillain visited southern Somali ports and immediate hinterland, providing excellent descriptions of the local political situation.

1854	In the course of his famous expedition to the Muslim city state of Harar on the edge of the Ethiopian escarpment, British Arabist and explorer Richard Burton spent several months on the northern Somali coast, between Berbera and Zeila. His *First Footsteps in East Africa* contains detailed and accurate information on Somali society and culture in this period. Burton memorably described the Somalis as a 'fierce and turbulent race of republicans'.
1860-97	Imperial partition of the Somali nation. Following the short-lived Egyptian colonisation of northern Somali coast, Britain, France and Italy signed 'protection' treaties with various Somali clans and partitioned the whole area with Ethiopia.
1900-1920	Seyyid Mohamed Abdille Hassan (the 'Mad Mullah') led holy war against 'infidel' colonisers—especially Ethiopians and British.
1920	Invention by Osman Yusuf Kenadid of first script for oral Somali language.
1934	'Walwal incident'—confrontation between Italian and Ethiopian forces at Walwal in the Ogaden which sparked off Italo-Ethiopian war and led eventually to World War II.
1941	Allies defeat Italians and establish British Military Administration throughout Somali region, with exception of French Somaliland.

1943	Somali Youth League, first major Somali nationist party founded with aid of British Military Administration.
1946	British Foreign Secretary, Ernest Bevin proposed that Somalilands should remain united as a single state and prepared for self-government.
1950	After rejection of Bevin Plan, Somalia placed under UN Trusteeship, administered by Italy, with ten year mandate. British Somaliland reverted to its former protectorate status, and the Ogaden was returned to Ethiopian control.
26 June 1960	British Somaliland became independent.
1st July 1960	Italian Somalia became independent and joined with Somaliland to form Somali Republic (Somalia).
1963	Ogaden insurrection followed by brief outbreak of fighting between Somalia and Ethiopia.
1963-1967	Somali guerrilla campaign attempting to secure Somali independence from Kenya in Northeastern region.
21 October 1969	Military coup lead by army commander, General Mohamed Siyad Barre, overthrew civilian government of Mohamed Haji Ibrahim Egal. State becomes 'Somali Democratic Republic' (SDR), and embraces 'scientific socialism'—with USSR assistance.
1973/74	National literacy campaigns using Latin-character script for writing Somali.

1974	Catastrophic drought and famine lead to large displacement of northern Somali nomads to agricultural and fishing 'collectives' in southern Somalia.
1977	Djibouti (French Somaliland and then later designated by the French as French Coast of Afars&Issas) became independent under President Hassan Guleid, an ethnic Somali. Ogaden nationalists rebelled against an Ethiopia weakened by revolution following Haile Selassie's overthrow.
1977/78	Somali-Ethiopian war. Soviet Union changed sides to aid Ethiopia, and was replaced in Somalia by USA.
1978	Somali deafeat, followed by influx of hundreds of thousands of Somali refugees. Abortive *coup* against Siyad.
1982	Formation of Somali Salvation Democratic Front (Mijerteyn) guerrilla forces in northeast, and Somali National Movement (Isaq) in northwest. Both based in Ethiopia.
1988	Peace accord between Ethiopia and Somalia led to intensification of SNM struggle in northwest.
1990	Siyad's divide and rule policies, arming his allies with his Western-supplied equipment, to surpress his enemies led to general militarisation and disintegration of the Somali state.
January 1991	Siyad overthrown by United Somali Congress (Hawiye) guerrillas and chased out of Mogadishu by General Aideed. General 'clan-cleansing' of Mogadishu by USC forces killing or driving out members of Darod clans associated with Siyad. Followed by

	power struggle between USC leaders and Ali Mahdi.
May 1991	SNM declares 'Somaliland Republic' independent of Somalia and distances itself from southern conflict and devastation.
March 1992	Mogadishu ceasefire followed by gradual return of humanitarian agencies to relieve spreading famine in southern Somali war zone.
April 1992	First UN special envoy appointed with prospect of UN security force to protect aid workers.
October 1992	UN launched '100 day action programme' and UN special envoy was forced to resign because of his justified criticism of UN operations.
December 1992	UN Resolution 794 authorised use of all necessary means to secure humanitarian relief, and US-led operation Restore Hope, involving 30,000 US and other troops, began its peace-keeping role in Somalia.
Jan & Mar 1993	Peace-conferences in Addis Ababa. Leaders of militia groups signed agreements binding themselves to disarm and maintain peace, subject to heavy sanctions.
May 1993	Operation Restore Hope hands over to UNOSOM II under Security Council resolution 814, which provided for a multi-national force of 28,000 military personnel and 3,000 civilians.
5 June 1993	Aideed's forces ambushed Pakistani UN contingent, killing over 20 Blue Helmets. Admiral Howe, UN special envoy in charge

of UNOSOM II, declared Aideed a wanted outlaw and launched attacks on Aideed strongholds in Mogadishu. Aideed's forces retaliated with guerrilla campaign against UN troops.

APPENDIX I

UN SECURITY COUNCIL RESOLUTION 814

RESOLUTION 814 (1993) ADOPTED BY THE SECURITY COUNCIL AT ITS 3188TH MEETING ON 26 MARCH 1993

THE SECURITY COUNCIL,

REAFFIRMING its resolutions 733 (1992) of 23 January 1992, 746 (1992) of 17 March 1992, 751 (1992) of 24 April 1992, 767 (1992) of 27 July 1992, 775 (1992) of 28 August 1992, and 794 (1992) of 3 December 1992,

BEARING IN MIND General Assembly resolution 47/167 of 18 December 1992,

COMMENDING the efforts of Member States acting pursuant to resolution 794 (1992) to establish a secure environment for humanitarian relief operations in Somalia,

ACKNOWLEDGING the need for a prompt, smooth and phased transition from the Unified Task Force (UNITAF) to the expanded United Nations Operation in Somalia (UNOSOM II),

REGRETTING the continuing incidents of violence in Somalia and the threat they pose to the reconciliation process

DEPLORING the acts of violence against persons engaging in humanitarian efforts on behalf of the United Nations, States, and non-governmental organizations,

NOTING WITH DEEP REGRET AND CONCERN the continuing reports of widespread violations of international humanitarian law and the general absence of the rule of law in Somalia,

RECOGNIZING that the people of Somalia bear the ultimate

responsibility for national reconciliation and reconstruction of their own country,

ACKNOWLEDGING the fundamental importance of a comprehensive and effective programme for disarming Somali parties, including movements and factions,

NOTING the need for continued humanitarian relief assistance and for the rehabilitation of Somalia's political institutions and economy,

CONCERNED that the crippling famine and drought in Somalia, compounded by the civil strife, have caused massive destruction to the means of production and the natural and human resources of that country,

EXPRESSING its appreciation to the Organization of African Unity, the League of Arab States, the Organization of the Islamic Conference and the Non-Aligned Movement for their cooperation with, and support of, the efforts of the United Nations in Somalia,

FURTHER EXPRESSING its appreciation to all Member States which have made contributions to the Fund established pursuant to paragraph 11 of resolution 794 (1992) and to all those who have provided humanitarian assistance to Somalia,

COMMENDING the efforts, in difficult circumstances, of the initial United Nations Operation in Somalia (UNOSOM) established pursuant to resolution 751 (1992),

EXPRESSING its appreciation for the invaluable assistance the neighbouring countries have been providing to the international community in its efforts to restore peace and security in Somalia and to host large numbers of refugees displaced by the conflict and TAKING NOTE of the difficulties caused to them due to the presence of refugees in their territories,

CONVINCED that the restoration of law and order throughout Somalia would contribute to humanitarian relief operations, reconciliation and political settlement, as well as to the rehabilitation of Somalia's political institutions and economy,

CONVINCED ALSO of the need for broad-based consultations and deliberations to achieve reconciliation, agreement on the setting up of transitional government institutions and consensus on basic principles and steps leading to the establishment of representative democratic institutions,

RECOGNIZING that the re-establishment of local and regional administrative institutions is essential to the restoration of domestic tranquillity,

ENCOURAGING the Secretary-General and his Special Representative to continue and intensify their work at the national, regional and local levels, including and encouraging broad participation by all sectors of Somali society, to promote the process of political settlement and national reconciliation and to assist the people of Somalia in rehabilitating their political institutions and economy.

EXPRESSING its readiness to assist the people of Somalia, as appropriate, on a local, regional or national level, to participate in free and fair elections, with a view towards achieving and implementing a political settlement,

WELCOMING the progress made at the United Nations-sponsored Informal Preparatory Meeting on Somali Political Reconciliation in Addis Ababa from 4 to 15 January 1993, in particular the conclusion at that meeting of three agreements by the Somali parties, including movements and factions, and WELCOMING ALSO any progress made at the Conference on National Reconciliation which began in Addis Ababa on 15 March 1993,

EMPHASIZING the need for the Somali people, including movements and factions, to show the political will to achieve security, reconciliation and peace,

NOTING the reports of States concerned of 17 December 1992 (S/24976) and 19 January 1993 (S/25126) and of the Secretary-General of 19 December 1992 (S/24992) and 26 January 1993 (S/25168) on the implementation of resolution 794 (1992),

HAVING EXAMINED the report of the Secretary-General of 3 March 1993 (S/25354 and Add.1 and 2.),

WELCOMING the intention of the Secretary General to seek maximum economy and efficiency and to keep the size of the United Nations presence, both military and civilian, to the minimum necessary to fulfil its mandate,

DETERMINING that the situation in Somalia continues to threaten peace and security in the region,

A

1. APPROVES the report of the Secretary-General of 3 March 1993;

2. EXPRESSES its appreciation to the Secretary-General for convening the Conference on National Reconciliation for Somalia in accordance with the agreements reached during the Informal Preparatory Meeting on Somali Political Reconciliation in Addis Ababa in January 1993 and for the progress achieved towards political reconciliation in Somalia, and also for his efforts to ensure that, as appropriate, all Somalis, including movements, factions, community leaders, women, professionals, intellectual, elders and other representative groups are suitably represented at such conferences;

3. WELCOMES the convening of the Third United Nations Coordination Meeting for Humanitarian Assistance for Somalia in Addis Ababa from 11 to 13 March 1993 and the willingness expressed by Governments through this process to contribute to relief and rehabilitation efforts in Somalia, where and when possible;

4. REQUESTS the Secretary-General, through his Special Representative, and with assistance, as appropriate, from all relevant United Nations entities, offices and specialized agencies, to provide humanitarian and other assistance to the people of Somalia in rehabilitating their political institutions and economy and promoting political settlement and national recon-

ciliation, in accordance with the recommendations contained in his report of 3 March 1993, including in particular:

(a) To assist in the provision of relief and in the economic rehabilitation of Somalia, based on an assessment of clear, prioritized needs, and taking into account, as appropriate, the 1993 Relief and Rehabilitation Programme for Somalia prepared by the United Nations Department of Humanitarian Affairs;

(b) To assist in the repatriation of refugees and displaced persons within Somalia;

(c) To assist the people of Somalia to promote and advance political reconciliation, through broad participation by all sectors of Somali society, and the re-establishment of national and regional institutions and civil administration in the entire country;

(d) To assist the re-establishment of Somali police, as appropriate at the local, regional or national level, to assist in the restoration and maintenance of peace, stability and law and order, including in the investigation and facilitating the prosecution of serious violations of international humanitarian law;

(e) To assist in the people of Somalia in the development of a coherent and integrated programme for the removal of mines throughout Somalia;

(f) To develop appropriate public information activities in support of the United Nations activities in Somalia;

(g) To create conditions under which Somali civil society may have a role, at every level, in the process of political reconciliation and in the formulation and realization of rehabilitation and reconstruction programmes;

B

ACTING under Chapter VII of the Charter of the United Nations,

5. DECIDED to expand the size of the UNOSOM force and its mandate in accordance with the recommendations contained in paragraphs 56-88 of the report of the Secretary-General of 3 March 1993, and the provisions of this resolution;

6. AUTHORIZES the mandate for the expanded UNOSOM

(UNOSOM II) for an initial period through 31 October 1993, unless previously renewed by the Security Council;

7 EMPHASIZES the crucial importance of disarmament and the urgent need to build on the efforts of UNITAF in accordance with paragraphs 56-69 of the report of the Secretary-General of 3 March 1993;

8. DEMANDS that all Somali parties, including movements and factions, comply fully with the commitments they have undertaken in the agreements they concluded at the Informal Preparatory Meeting on Somali Political Reconciliation in Addis Ababa, and in particular with their Agreement on Implementing the Cease-fire and on Modalities of Disarmament (S/25168, annex III);

9. FURTHER DEMANDS that all Somali parties, including movements and factions, take all measures to ensure the safety of the personnel of the United Nations and its agencies as well as the staff of the International Committee of the Red Cross (ICRC), intergovernmental organizations and non-governmental organizations engaged in providing humanitarian and other assistance to the people of Somalia in rehabilitating their political institutions and economy and promoting political settlement and national reconciliation;

10. REQUESTS the Secretary-General to support from within Somalia the implementation of the arms embargo established by resolution 733 (1992), utilizing as available and appropriate the UNOSOM II forces authorized by this resolution, and to report on this subject, with any recommendations regarding more effective measures if necessary, to the Security Council;

11. CALLS UPON all States, in particular neighbouring States, to cooperate in the implementation of the arms embargo established by resolution 733 (1992);

12. REQUESTS the Secretary-General to provide security, as appropriate, to assist in the repatriation of refugees and the assisted resettlement of displaced persons, utilizing UNOSOM II forces, paying particular attention to those areas where major

instability continues to threaten peace and security in the region;

13. REITERATES ITS DEMAND that all Somali parties, including movements and factions, immediately cease and desist from all breaches of international humanitarian law and REAFFIRMS that those responsible for such acts be held individually accountable;

14. REQUESTS the Secretary-General, through his Special Representative, to direct the Force Commander of UNOSOM II to assume responsibility for the consolidation, expansion and maintenance of a secure environment throughout Somalia, taking account of the particular circumstances in each locality, on an expedited basis in accordance with the recommendations contained in his report of 3 March 1993, and in this regard to organize a prompt, smooth and phased transition from UNITAF to UNOSOM II;

15. REQUESTS the Secretary-General to maintain the fund established pursuant to resolution 794 (1992) for additional purpose of receiving contributions for maintenance of UNOSOM II forces following the departure of UNITAF forces and for the establishment of Somali police, and calls on Member States to make contributions to this fund, in addition to their assessed contributions;

16. EXPRESSES APPRECIATION to the United Nations agencies, intergovernmental and non-governmental organizations and the ICRC for their contributions and assistance and REQUESTS the Secretary-General to ask them to continue to extend financial, material and technical support to the Somali people in all regions of the country;

17. REQUESTS the Secretary-General to seek, as appropriate, pledges and contributions from States and others to assist in financing the rehabilitation of the political institutions and economy of Somalia;

18. REQUESTS the Secretary-General to keep the Security Council fully informed on action taken to implement the present

resolution, in particular to submit as soon as possible a report to the Council containing recommendations for establishment of Somali police forces and thereafter to report no later than every ninety days on the progress achieved in accomplishing the objectives set out in the present resolutions;

19. DECIDES to conduct a formal review of the progress towards accomplishing the purposes of the present resolution no later than 31 October 1993;

20. DECIDES to remain actively seized of the matter.

APPENDIX II

ADDIS ABABA AGREEMENTS

AGREEMENTS OF THE FIRST SESSION OF THE CONFERENCE ON NA-
TIONAL RECONCILIATION IN SOMALIA, 27 MARCH 1993

After long and costly years of civil war that ravaged our
country, plunged it into famine, and caused acute suffering and
loss of life among our people, there is the light of hope at last;
progress has been made towards the restoration of peace,
security and reconciliation in Somalia.

We the Somali political leaders, recognise how vital it is that
this process continue, it has our full commitment. By our atten-
dance at this historic conference, we have resolved to put an end
to armed conflict and to reconcile our differences through peaceful means. We pledge to consolidate and carry forward advances
in peace, security and dialogue made since the beginning of this
year. National reconciliation is now the most fervent wish of the
Somali people.

We commit ourselves to continuing the peace process under
the auspices of the United Nations and in cooperation with the
Regional Organizations and the Standing Committee of the
Horn as well as with our neighbors in the Horn of Africa.

After an era of pain, destruction and bloodshed that turned
Somalis against Somalis, we have confronted our respon-
sibilities. We now pledge to work towards the rebirth of Somalia,
to restore its dignity as a country and rightful place in the Community of Nations. At the close of the Holy Month of Ramadan,
we believe this is the most precious gift we can give to our people.

The serenity and shade of a tree, which according to our
Somali tradition is a place of reverence and rapprochement, has
been replaced by the conference hall. Yet the promises made here
are no less sacred or binding.

Therefore, we the undersigned Somali political leaders, meeting at Africa Hall in Addis Ababa, Ethiopia between 15 and 27

March 1993, hereby reaffirm our commitment to the agreements signed during the Informal Preparatory Meeting on National Reconciliation in January 1993.

In concord to end hostilities, and to build on the foundation of peace for reconstruction and rehabilitation in Somalia, we agree to proceed within the framework of the following provisions and decisions:

I. DISARMAMENT AND SECURITY:

1 AFFIRM that uprooting of banditry and crime is necessary for peace, stability, security, reconciliation, reconstruction and development in Somalia;

2 FURTHER AFFIRM that disarmament must and shall be comprehensive, impartial and transparent;

3 COMMIT ourselves to complete, and simultaneous disarmament throughout the entire country in accordance with the disarmament concepts and timeframe set by the Cease-fire Agreement of January 1993, and request that UNITAF/UNOSOM assist these efforts so as to achieve a substantial completion of the disarmament within 90 days;

4 FURTHER REITERATE our commitment to the strict, effective and expeditious implementation of the Cease-fire/Disarmament Agreement signed on 8 and 15 January 1993;

5 AFFIRM our commitment to comply with the requirements of the Cease-fire Agreements signed in January of 1993, including the total and complete hand-over of weapons to UNITAF/UNOSOM;

6 URGE UNITAF/UNOSOM to apply strong and effective sanctions against those responsible for any violation of the Cease-fire Agreement of January 1993;

7 STRESS the need for the air, sea and land borders of Somalia to be closely guarded by UNITAF/UNOSOM in order to prevent any flow of arms into the country and to prevent violation of the territorial waters of Somalia;

II. REHABILITATION AND RECONSTRUCTION:

1. AFFIRM the need to accelerate the supply and operation of relief, reconstruction and rehabilitation programs in Somalia;

2. WELCOME the conclusion of the Third Coordination Meeting on Humanitarian Assistance to Somalia;

3. EXPRESS our appreciation to donor countries for their continued humanitarian assistance to Somalia and, in particular, for the generous pledge, made at the Third Coordination Meeting, to mobilize $142 million for relief and rehabilitation efforts in Somalia.

4. CALL UPON UNOSOM, aid agencies and donor countries to immediately assist in the rehabilitation of essential public and social services, and of necessary infrastructure, on a priority basis by the end of June 1993;

5. ASSURE the international community of the full desire of Somali leaders to re-establish, with the assistance of UNOSOM, a secure environment for relief, reconstruction and rehabilitation operations and the protection of relief and rehabilitation workers and supplies;

6. CONDEMN the acts of violence committed against relief workers and all forms of extortion regarding humanitarian operations;

7. URGE the organizations within the UN system and NGOs to effectively utilize Somali human resources in the rehabilitation and reconstruction process in Somalia.

III. RESTORATION OF PROPERTY AND SETTLEMENT OF DISPUTES:

1. AFFIRM that all disputes must henceforth be settled by dialogue, negotiations and other peaceful and legal means;

2. FURTHER AFFIRM that all private or public properties that were illegally confiscated, robbed, stolen, seized, embezzled or taken by other fraudulent means must be returned to their rightful owners;

3. DECIDE to deal with this matter within the framework specified in the report of the committee on the peaceful settlement of disputes.

IV. TRANSITIONAL MECHANISMS:

1. The Somali people believe that there is concurrence among the people of Somalia that Somalia must retain its rightful place

in the community of nations and that they must express their political views and make the decisions that affect them. This is an essential component of the search for peace.

To achieve this, political and administrative structures in Somalia need to be rebuilt to provide the people as a whole with an opportunity to participate in shaping the future of the country.

In this context, the establishment of transitional mechanisms which prepare the country for a stable and democratic future is absolutely essential. During the transitional period, which will last for a period of two years effective from the date of signature to this agreement, the emphasis will be upon the provision of essential services, complete disarmament, restoration of peace and domestic tranquility and on the attainment of the reconciliation of the Somali people. Emphasis will also be put on the rehabilitation and reconstruction of basic infrastructure and on the building of democratic institutions. All of this will prepare the country to enter a constitutional phase in which the institutions of democratic governance, rule of law, decentralization of power, protection of human rights and individual liberties, and the safeguarding of the integrity of the Somali Republic are all in place.

Therefore, we have agreed to a broad outline of a framework for a transitional system or governance to allow for the provision of essential services, the creation of a basis for long-term planning, and for the resumption of greater administrative responsibility by Somalia. In general terms, this system will be composed of four basic administrative components that will be mandated to function during the transitional period.

Taking into account the reality of the situation in Somalia today and the need for stability, we hereby agree to the establishment of the following four basic transitional organs of authority:

1. The Transitional National Council (TNC)

The TNC will:

a) be the repository of Somali sovereignty;

b) be the prime political authority having legislative functions during the period in question;

c) interact, as appropriate, with the international community, including UNOSOM;

d) appoint various committees, including the Transitional Charter Drafting Committee, as required;

e) appoint Officers for its various functions;

f) appoint the heads of administrative departments;

g) oversee the performance of the departments created; and

h) establish an independent Judiciary.

The TNC shall be composed of:

a) Three representatives from each of the 18 regions currently recognized, including one woman from each region;

b) Five additional seats from Mogadishu;

c) One nominee from each of the political factions currently participating in the First session of the National Reconciliation Conference.

2. *The Central Administrative Departments (CADs)*

The TNC will appoint the heads of the Central Administrative Departments, whose prime function will be to re-establish and operate the departments of civil administration, social affairs, economic affairs and humanitarian affairs, paving the way for the re-establishment and operation of a formal government. The CADs shall comprise skilled professionals having the ability to reinstate, gradually, the administrative functions of national public administration. The performance of these departments will be overseen by the TNC.

3. *Regional Councils (RCs)*

Regional Councils shall be established in all the existing 18 regions of Somalia. The present 18 regions shall be maintained during the transitional period. The Regional Councils shall be entrusted primarily with the task of implementing humanitarian, social and economic programs in coordination with the TNC and will also assist in the conducting of the internationally-supervised census. The Regional Councils will liaise with UNOSOM II, UN specialized agencies, NGOs and other relevant organizations directly and through the Central Administrative Departments and Transitional National Council. The Regional Councils shall also be responsible for law and order at the regional level. In this regard, the law enforcement institutions will be a regional police force and a regional judiciary. The District Councils (see below) in each region shall send representatives who will constitute the Regional Councils.

4. District Councils

District Councils shall be established in the present districts in every region. District council members shall be appointed through election or through consensus-based selection in accordance with Somali traditions. The District Councils shall be responsible for managing the affairs of the district including public safety, health, education and reconstruction.

V. CONCLUSIONS:

The Conference agreed on the appointment, by the TNC, of a Transitional Charter Drafting Committee referred to in section IV. 1. (d) above. In drafting the Transitional Charter, the Committee shall be guided by the basic principles of the Universal Declaration of Human Rights and by the Somali traditional ethics.

The Conference agreed that the TNC shall appoint a "Peace Delegation" composed of political movements and other social elements to travel to all parts of the country for the purpose of advancing the peace and reconciliation process as well as to explain the agreements reached in Addis Ababa.

We further agree that the TNC shall appoint a National Committee to bring about reconciliation and seek solutions to outstanding political problems with the SNM.

The Conference also calls upon the international community and in particular on the neighboring states to facilitate the noble effort at reconciliation by providing moral and material support.

In conclusion, we the undersigned, in agreeing to the above, resolve that never again will Somalia suffer the tragedy of the recent past. Emerging from the darkness of catastrophe and war, we Somalis herald the beginning of a new era of peace, of healing and rebuilding, in which cooperation and trust will overcome hatred and suspicion. It is a message we must pass on to our children and our grandchildren so that the proud Somali family, as we knew it, can once again become whole.

We, the undersigned, hereby pledge to abandon the logic of force for the ethic of dialogue. We will pursue the process of national reconciliation with vigor and sincerity, in accordance with this declaration and with the cooperation of the people of Somalia as a whole.

Recognizing the tragic and painful recent history of problems in our country, we pledge to achieve comprehensive national reconciliation through peaceful means. We also pledge to adopt, in all parts of Somalia, transitional measures that will contribute to harmony and healing of wounds among all the people of Somalia.

We invite the Secretary-General of the United Nations and his Special Representative in Somalia, in accordance with the mandate entrusted to them by the UN Security Council, to extend all necessary assistance to the people of Somalia for the implementation of this agreement.

AGREEMENT REACHED BETWEEN THE POLITICAL LEADERS AT THE (SECOND SESSION) CONSULTATIONS HELD IN ADDIS ABABA, 30 MARCH 1993

1. For the formation of the Transitional National Council (TNC) each faction will nominate a representative.

2. Given the 18 regions three representatives will be chosen by each region and names will be submitted to UNOSOM by the factions.

3. In regions where there are more than one faction or differences between the factions in the allocation of the seats the concerned factions will try to settle their differences in Addis Ababa, if not, they will iron out their differences in the regions.

4. Criteria for the selection of TNC members:

  (a) Somali citizen;

  (b) Not less than 30 years of age;

  (c) The person should be mentally fit;

  (d) The person should be literate;

  (e) The nomination of the TNC members should be completed within 45 days as of 1 April 1993;

  (f) UNOSOM will provide the logistical support and act as observer where there are disputes;

5. Committee: In view of the time factor a committee will be set up to draft the charter which will be approved and adopted by the TNC. The first session of this drafting committee will start on the 10 April 1993 in Mogadishu. The composition of the Charter Committee will be:

  (a) Two members nominated by each political faction—one with political experience and another with legal experience;

  (b) International and legal advisors should be provided by UNOSOM;

  (c) UNOSOM should provide the financial resource for the work of the Committee. The Charter should be completed within 45 days starting 10 April 1993. The Drafting Committee will work in Mogadishu.

DISARMAMENT

It was agreed that the disarmament process will be fully implemented.

International participation through UNOSOM is necessary, this will include reconstruction and rehabilitation, humanitarian assistance, development, logistical support, communications, security, de-mining and mobilization throughout Somalia.

It was also agreed that an official delegation comprising of one member from each faction led by General Mohammed Farah Aideed will go to SNM and will report to the TNC. All expenses, logistics and security related to the work of this good-will mission will be paid by UNOSOM.

[Signatories to both documents were as follows:

SAMO, Mohamed R. Arbow; SDA, Mohamed F. Abdullahi; SDM, Abdi Musse Mayow; SDM(SNA), Mohamed Nur Alio; SNDU, Ali Ismail Abdi; SNF, Gen. Omar Haji Mohamed; SNU, Mohamed Rajis Mohamed; SPM, Gen. Aden Abdullahi Nur; SPM(SNA), Ahmed Hashi Mahmmud; SSDF, Gen. Mohammed Abshir Mussa; SSNM, Abdi Warsame Isaq; USC(SNA), Gen. Mohammed Farah Aidid; USC, Mohammed Qanyare Afrah; USF, Abdurahman Dualeh Ali; USP, Mohamed Abdi Hashi.]

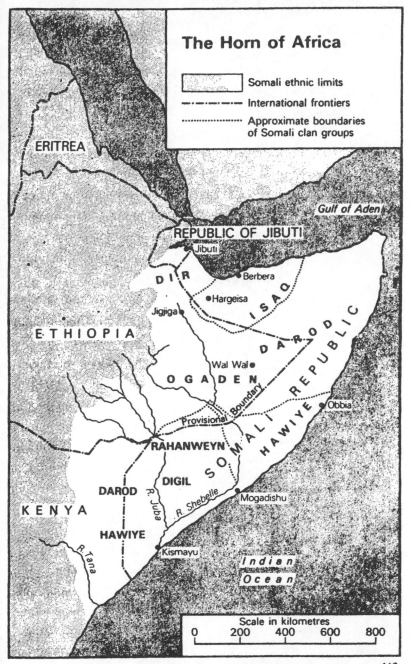

The Horn of Africa

Legend:
- Somali ethnic limits
- International frontiers
- Approximate boundaries of Somali clan groups

ERITREA

Gulf of Aden

REPUBLIC OF JIBUTI

Jibuti

Berbera

DIR

Hargeisa

ISAQ

Jigiiga

DAROD

ETHIOPIA

Wal Wal

OGADEN

REPUBLIC

Provisional

Boundary

Obbia

HAWIYE

SOMALI

RAHANWEYN

DIGIL

DAROD

R. Juba

R. Shebelle

Mogadishu

KENYA

HAWIYE

R. Tana

Kismayu

Indian Ocean

Scale in kilometres

0   200   400   600   800

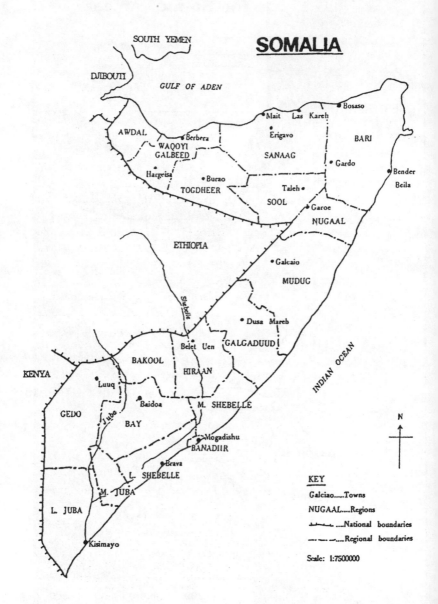

SOMALIA

SOUTH YEMEN

DJIBOUTI

GULF OF ADEN

• Bosaso

• Mait   Las Kareh

AWDAL

• Berbera

• Erigavo

BARI

WAQOYI
GALBEED

SANAAG

• Gardo

• Bender
Beila

Hargeisa

• Burao

TOGDHEER

• Taleh

SOOL

• Garoe

NUGAAL

ETHIOPIA

• Galcaio

MUDUG

Shebelle

• Dusa Mareb

Belet Uen

GALGADUUD

BAKOOL

HIRAAN

KENYA

• Luuq

Juba

• Baidoa

M. SHEBELLE

GEDO

BAY

• Mogadishu

BANADIIR

• Brava

L. SHEBELLE

M. JUBA

L. JUBA

• Kisimayo

INDIAN OCEAN

N

KEY

Galciao.....Towns

NUGAAL.....Regions

⊢⊣⊢⊣ ...National boundaries

—·—·— ...Regional boundaries

Scale: 1:7500000

114

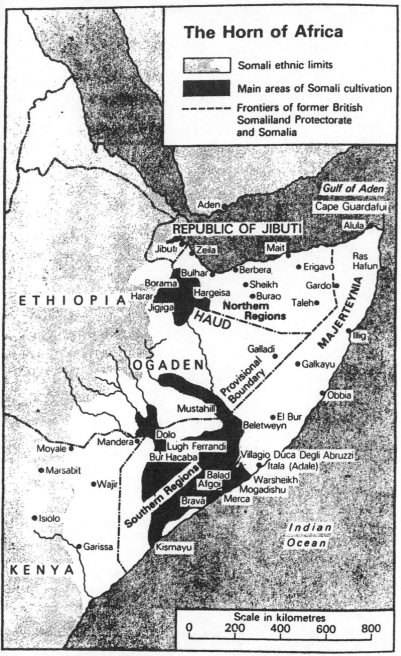

The Horn of Africa

- Somali ethnic limits
- Main areas of Somali cultivation
- - - - - Frontiers of former British Somaliland Protectorate and Somalia

Gulf of Aden

Aden

Cape Guardafui

REPUBLIC OF JIBUTI

Alula

Jibuti · Zeila · Mait

Ras Hafun

Bulhar · Berbera · Erigavo

Borama

Hargeisa · Sheikh

Gardo

ETHIOPIA Harar

Burao

Taleh·

Jigjiga

Northern
Regions

HAUD

MAJERTEYNIA

Illig·

OGADEN

Galladi

Provisional
Boundary

· Galkayu

Obbia·

Mustahill

· El Bur

Beletweyn

Moyale·

Mandera·

Dolo
Lugh Ferrandi
Bur Hacaba

Villagio Duca Degli Abruzzi
Itala (Adale)

· Marsabit

·Wajir

Balad
Afgoi

Warsheikh
Mogadishu

Southern Regions

Bravá

Merca

· Isiolo

Indian
Ocean

· Garissa

KENYA

Kismayu

Scale in kilometres

0   200   400   600   800